D1307280

Chef Belinda has done it again, following the success of her classic *Just Peachy*, with this inspired collection of recipes for everyone's favorite meal. *Let's Brunch* is full of scrumptious dishes but, more importantly, the recipes are very user-friendly for cooks of all skill levels. You will want a copy for your own kitchen shelves, but will also want to gift it to your friends and family.

Peter Reinhart, author of *Perfect Pan Pizza* and *The Bread Baker's Apprentice*

A happy, relaxed host who is excited to gather family and friends around the table and feed them well is the heart and soul of gracious hospitality. In that spirit, Chef Belinda shares 100 signature recipes for brunch, her favorite way to entertain. Belinda's enthusiasm and experience will inspire us to prepare and share a delicious brunch with confidence, and have fun with it.

Sheri Castle, Food Writer and Cooking Teacher

Staying in for brunch is destined to become fashionable when these stellar recipes by Belinda Smith-Sullivan appear on your table. Savory or sweet, mild or spicy, vegetarian or omnivore, there's a great dish awaiting every palate and pleasure. Serving recipes from *Let's Brunch* will make you a star!

Cynthia Graubart, James Beard Foundation Award-winning cookbook author

Belinda Smith-Sullivan applies her classy touch to one of the best occasions for gathering with friends. With recipes that can stretch from breakfast to lunch or (oh, lucky day) dinner, or even travel to someone else's brunch, her collection will be there for those special days with family and friends.

Kathleen Purvis, Charlotte-based food writer

Let's Brunch is an irresistible invitation to celebrate with friends and family in the sunny heart of the day. From Croque Madame and New Orleans-Style Barbecue Shrimp to Crab Louie Salad and Breakfast Macaroni and Cheese, Chef Belinda's deliciously doable recipes hand us the key to memorable gatherings at home. I can't wait to cook up happy times from this beautiful book.

Nancie McDermott, food blogger and author of
The Wok & Skillet Cookbook: 300 Recipes for Stir-Frys & Noodles

Let's Brunch

100 RECIPES FOR THE BEST MEAL OF THE WEEK

BELINDA SMITH-SULLIVAN

Photographs by Susan Barnson Hayward

GIBBS SMITH
TO ENRICH AND INSPIRE HUMANKIND

Acknowledgments

Michelle Branson and the *entire* Gibbs Smith Team for your vote of confidence . . . again!

Martha Hopkins of Terrace Partners, my agent, for your dedication, guidance, and patience. You keep me focused.

Kathleen, Jeanne, Linda, Dede, Lisa, and Lily for that push across the finish line that I so desperately needed! Thank you for your friendship, support, and encouragement.

The Augusta Gourmet Club, for being my forever champions!

All my neighbors, friends, and family who served themselves up as my taste-testers.

Foreword

Belinda Smith-Sullivan has become one of the South's great recipe developers and cookbook authors on the strength of her exceptionally fine sense of balance and her prodigious energy, turning the ripe orchard peach into a whole rhapsody on the fruit entitled *Just Peachy*, which incorporates ancient farmstead traditions and modern culinary practice in 70 delicious and finely-tuned recipes.

She is—no surprise—the perfect person to attack the weekend's great comfort-food meal and find both fresh ideas and wonderful heirlooms worth celebrating. We hope you will be inspired as we are by Smith-Sullivan's recipes and words and by Susan Barnson Hayward's ravishing photos in *Let's Brunch*!

— Matt Lee and Ted Lee, authors of
The Lee Bros. Charleston Kitchen

Introduction

We are becoming a "brunch culture." Be it brunch *à deux,* a brunch buffet, or a group of friends hanging out on the patio around a harvest table, eating frittatas and drinking Bellini's, it is a concept that is here to stay!

In my opinion, brunch is the most creative meal because there are no rules—as menu offerings can range from a full array of breakfast items to steak and potatoes and everything in between. It's why more and more restaurants serve breakfast, lunch, and dinner simultaneously all throughout the day. I prefer brunch as an entertainment option because it is and always has been "entertaining lite." The ingredients and beverages are usually very simple. You are not competing for guests' time—who usually have several invitations and commitments for their Friday and Saturday nights. And the hosts and guests are more relaxed.

For me it all started in New York years ago when I lived in a six-floor walkup apartment. I could get friends to come every Sunday and climb the endless stairs for a champagne brunch—that, by the way, did not break the bank!

Fast forward many years to culinary school. Of the many experiences I was exposed to, cooking techniques, international cuisines, food science, butchering skills, nutrition, food safety, and etc., one of my favorite experiences was my externship at the Marriott in Charlotte, North Carolina. I was a prep cook, which meant I spent nine hours a day peeling, chopping, slicing, and cutting up stuff. There were days when I would prep several cases each of cantaloupes, pineapples, and honeydew melons, not to mention dipping over 500 strawberries in chocolate, in addition to all of my other duties. This lasted for weeks until I caught my big break—the opportunity to work the omelet and waffle station in the dining room during a Sunday brunch!

The excitement lasted all of ten minutes until I learned working that position meant I had to arrive at 5 a.m. to cook speed racks full of bacon and sausages and giant-size pots of grits and oatmeal. Only then would I have the privilege of standing, for four hours, in the middle of the dining room flipping omelets and making waffles.

On my first day at the omelet station, it became evident to me why what I did as a prep cook was so important. The dining room was packed, the buffet was stuffed with everything imaginable to eat, and there was a high level of energy and laughter around the room. And in the years since my externship, I have witnessed this same energy in brunch settings everywhere. This is evidence of the popularity of brunch—it just makes you happy!

But to what can we attribute this Sunday madness we call brunch; a blend of the words "breakfast and lunch?" The theories abound. Some think it is a tradition that started as far back as the late nineteenth century and has roots in England's lavish, multi-course hunt breakfasts. Others assume that it derived from the practice of Catholics fasting before Sunday mass and communion then returning home to feast on a large midday meal.

The tradition caught on in the United States before WWII when transcontinental trains stopped in Chicago to allow passengers to enjoy a late Sunday morning meal offered by many local hotels.

Restaurants, that were closed on Sundays, soon began offering decadent spreads accompanied by signature morning cocktails like mimosas, Bloody Marys and Bellinis. Also, after WWII, many women entered the workforce and brunch was a way to give these working wives and mothers a much needed relief from cooking on Sundays. Thus, the rise in the popularity of the Sunday brunch.

Brunch has been a tradition in the south for many years. It was a way to fellowship after attending church service on Sundays, and it still is a way for bringing people together.

Just observe the long lines and wait periods trying to get into your favorite restaurant on Sunday afternoon. No doubt about it, going out to brunch is a treat you give to yourself. But inviting friends and family into your home for a warm and inviting brunch is a shared and cherished experience for everyone.

Brunch is proving to be ever evolving. With the elevated interest in sports-going, brunch has even manifested itself in stadium parking lots in advance of game time. Not to mention food trucks that have forged a way for themselves into this fray. There is no end to where this "brunch culture" is taking us! Whether it's to honor Mother's Day, a cooking break during the holidays, or to sweep away the cobwebs of a long week.

Brunch just might become the new dinner party.
Celebrate it!

Breads & Toppings

Sweet Potato Buttermilk Biscuits

MAKES 14 TO 16 BISCUITS

This biscuit is on the sweeter side of regular biscuits. But who could resist using one of the south's most popular vegetables—the sweet potato?

Preheat oven to 425 degrees F. Prepare a baking sheet or 12-inch cast iron skillet with a light spray of nonstick cooking spray.

Into the bowl of a food processor fitted with the dough blade, add flour, cinnamon, and sugar and stir together. Add butter and shortening and pulse just until the butter pieces are about the size of small peas (5–7 pulses).

Pour into a large bowl, make a well in the center of the flour, and add sweet potato purée and buttermilk to the well. Using a spatula, or your fingers, in a circular motion, fold the flour into wet mixture. Mix just enough until a dough ball forms. Do not overmix. Turn dough out onto a clean, floured surface.

Using floured hands, pat dough into a round disk about $1/2$-thick and fold in half. Repeat this step 2 more times. (Keep the surface floured.) Then pat dough into a disk $1/2$ inch thick for normal biscuits or $3/4$ inch for tall biscuits. Using a 2-inch biscuit cutter dipped into flour, cut out biscuits starting at the outside of the dough and working your way to the center. Combine leftover scraps to form additional biscuits. Place cut biscuits onto baking sheet or in cast iron skillet, and bake for 10–15 minutes until lightly brown. Serve hot.

2 cups self-rising flour

$1/4$ teaspoon cinnamon

$1/4$ cup light brown sugar

$1/4$ cup unsalted butter, cut into $1/2$-inch cubes and chilled

$1/4$ cup shortening, cut into $1/2$-inch cubes and chilled

1 cup sweet potato purée or canned pumpkin

$1/2$ cup buttermilk

Ramp Buttermilk Biscuits

2 cups self-rising flour

¼ cup unsalted butter, cubed and chilled

¼ cup shortening, cubed and chilled

½ cup chopped ramps

1 cup buttermilk

Southerners know biscuits, and what they are most emphatic about are buttermilk biscuits! Pair them with some gravy and you've got a match made in heaven. Ramps are wild onions found mostly in the Southeast and along the eastern coastline. Sometimes called spring onions, wild leeks, or wild garlic, ramps closely resemble scallions, with a white bulb and leafy stalk. If unable to source ramps in your area, substitute leeks, scallions, or chives.

Preheat oven to 425 degrees F. Prepare a baking sheet with a light spray of nonstick cooking spray.

Measure flour into a large mixing bowl and, using a pastry cutter, 2 knives, or your clean hands, cut in butter and shortening until it resembles small peas. Or if you are using a food processor, pulse a few times until the consistency is achieved.

Evenly distribute the ramps over the flour mixture and, using a spatula, add in buttermilk and mix just until combined. Do not overmix the dough. Turn the dough onto a floured cutting board or countertop. Using floured hands, gently pat (do not use a rolling pin) the dough until it is ½ inch thick. Fold in half and pat down again and repeat 1 more time.

Use a 2-inch round cookie cutter or biscuit cutter to cut dough into rounds and place onto baking sheet. If you like soft sides, place biscuits touching each other. If you like crusty sides, place them about 1 inch apart. They will not rise as high as the biscuits placed close together. Bake 10–15 minutes until golden brown. Serve hot.

Panettone Grand Marnier French Toast

SERVES 6 TO 8

Panettone is an Italian sweetbread loaf, similar to an American fruit-cake, but a lot lighter, less sweet, and less dense in texture. It is good toasted with butter and a minimal amount of jam for a light breakfast snack or sliced thick and used to make a delicious fruit and nut-filled French toast. It is widely sold in supermarkets and specialty food outlets starting in the fall through New Year's and during Easter. This dish is a special brunch choice and treat during the holiday season. Panettone would also be an excellent choice used in a holiday bread pudding.

4 large eggs

1 cup heavy cream

1 tablespoon sugar

¼ cup Grand Marnier

1 teaspoon orange zest

½ teaspoon ground cardamom

1 teaspoon vanilla or almond extract

Pinch of kosher salt

1 loaf panettone, sliced crossways into 1-inch slices

Unsalted butter for griddle, plus additional

Assorted fresh-cut berries, optional

Whipped cream, for garnish

Powdered sugar, for garnish

Syrup, of choice

Whisk together eggs, cream, sugar, Grand Marnier, orange zest, cardamom, vanilla, and salt. Pour into a shallow dish. Dip the panettone slices in the mixture and place on a flat dish. Let rest for 15 minutes until the egg mixture is absorbed.

Preheat oven to 200 degrees F. Heat griddle over medium heat, and melt 2 tablespoons butter. Working in batches, add 3 to 4 slices of batter-soaked bread to griddle and cook until brown on both sides. Keep adding butter as needed. Move cooked toast to a baking sheet and keep warm in oven. Repeat until all slices are cooked.

To serve, transfer to serving plates, add fruit, whipped cream, and garnish with powdered sugar. Add butter and syrup as needed.

Hot Cross Buns

MAKES 12 TO 14 BUNS

Dough

¼ cup apple juice

½ cup dried fruit, of choice

½ cup raisins or dried currants

1¼ cups milk, room temperature

2 large eggs, room temperature

1 egg yolk, reserve white

6 tablespoons unsalted butter, room temperature

2 teaspoons instant yeast*

¼ cup firmly packed light brown sugar

1 teaspoon ground cardamom

¼ teaspoon ground cinnamon

¼ teaspoon ground cloves

1¾ teaspoons kosher salt

1 tablespoon baking powder

4½ cups all-purpose flour

Hot Cross Buns are an Easter brunch tradition! Made with a rich yeast dough containing a variety of fruits and warming spices, they are marked on top with a cross, either cut into the dough or with strips of pastry or piped with a thick icing. Either way you finish them, your family is sure to enjoy them as they are reminded of the nursery rhyme that inspired this sweet treat.

"Hot Cross Buns! Hot Cross Buns!
One a penny, two a penny, Hot Cross Buns!
If you have no daughters, give them to your sons,
One a penny, two a penny, Hot Cross Buns!

In a medium bowl, mix together apple juice with the dried fruit and raisins. Cover with plastic wrap and microwave briefly, just until the fruit and liquid are very warm, about 1 minute. Set aside to cool to room temperature. In the bowl of a stand mixer using the dough hook, mix together milk, eggs, egg yolk, butter, yeast, sugar, spices, salt, baking powder, and flour; knead until the dough is soft and elastic (check manufacturer's instructions for setting). Mix in the cooled fruit and any liquid left in the bowl. Cover the bowl with a clean dish towel and let the dough rise for 1 hour. It should become puffy, though may not double in bulk.

*Not to be confused with dry active yeast. Instant yeast is mixed in with all of the other dry ingredients and does not require proofing (mixing with water).

Lightly spray a 10-inch square pan or 9 x 13-inch pan with cooking spray. Using a 3–4 ounce muffin scoop, divide the dough into 12–14 billiard ball-size pieces. Use clean, greased hands to round them into balls. Arrange them in the prepared pan.

Cover the pan, and let the buns rise for 1 hour, or until they've puffed up and are touching one another.

While the dough is rising, preheat the oven to 375 degrees F. In a small bowl, whisk together the egg white and milk, and brush over the buns, just before putting in the oven. Bake the buns for 20 minutes until golden brown. Remove from the oven and transfer to a wire rack.

In a medium bowl, mix together powdered sugar, vanilla, salt, and milk into a thick icing and place in a piping bag or a small plastic ziptop bag with corner cut off to make an opening. When buns are completely cool, pipe a cross on top of each bun. Let rest until icing is set.

Topping

1 reserved egg white

1 tablespoon milk

Icing

1 cup plus 2 tablespoons powdered sugar

$1/2$ teaspoon vanilla extract

Pinch of kosher salt

4 teaspoons milk, more if needed

Brisket-Stuffed Herb Cornbread

SERVES APPROXIMATELY 12

1 cup cornmeal

1 cup all-purpose flour

1/2 tablespoon baking powder

1/2 teaspoon baking soda

2 tablespoons sugar

3/4 teaspoon kosher salt

2 large eggs

1 cup buttermilk

1 tablespoon chopped fresh thyme leaves

1 teaspoon chopped fresh rosemary

2 tablespoons vegetable oil

1 to 2 cups chopped Slow-Roasted Beet Brisket (page 140)

1 cup grated cheese, Gruyère or white cheddar

This takes the sandwich to a new height! A meat and bread option that requires no assembly—it comes out of the oven ready to enjoy. Wrap a few chunks in some plastic wrap and throw into a backpack along with a bottle of wine for an impromptu picnic brunch. The best of both worlds— cornbread and slow-roasted brisket. Does it get any better than this? Make it in a skillet and slice or in an oversize muffin tin as individual special treats.

Preheat oven to 400 degrees F. Prepare a 9- or 10-inch cast iron skillet with nonstick cooking spray.

In a large bowl, combine cornmeal, flour, baking powder, baking soda, sugar, and salt. In a medium bowl, whisk together eggs, buttermilk, herbs, and oil. Add to dry ingredients and mix well.

Pour half of batter into the skillet and spread evenly. Cover with brisket and grated cheese; add remaining batter on top. Bake for 25–30 minutes or until a cake tester, inserted into the thickest part of the cornbread, comes out clean. Let rest 10–15 minutes before slicing.

Rum, Date, and Walnut Bread

1 cup chopped pitted dates

4 tablespoons rum, divided

2 cups all-purpose flour

1/2 teaspoon baking powder

1/2 teaspoon baking soda

1/2 teaspoon kosher salt

1/2 cup sugar

1/2 cup brown sugar

2 large eggs, room temperature

2 tablespoons vegetable oil

1/2 cup plain Greek yogurt

1 cup chopped toasted walnut halves

Honey Butter (page 32)

This quick bread is versatile enough to be served as a mini breakfast with a smear of flavored butter or as a full-blown brunch accompaniment. It is equally as good as a dinner dessert with a scoop of ice cream on top.

Preheat oven to 350 degrees F. Prepare a 9 x 5-inch loaf pan with nonstick cooking spray.

In a medium bowl, soak dates in 2 tablespoons rum, stirring occasionally, for 30 minutes.

In a large bowl, combine flour, baking powder, baking soda, salt, and sugars. In medium bowl, whisk eggs, oil, remaining rum, and yogurt. Stir wet ingredients into dry and mix thoroughly. Add dates and nuts and stir just to combine.

Pour batter into prepared pan and bake for 60 minutes or until a cake tester, inserted into the middle, comes out clean. Remove from oven and cool in pan for 10 minutes. Remove from pan and cool completely on a wire rack before serving with Honey Butter.

Garlic-Infused Olive Oil

MAKES 1 PINT (2 CUPS)

Garlic-Infused Olive Oil is a timesaver in the kitchen and so easy to make. No more bits of minced garlic to bite into in your homemade salad dressings or on your roasted veggies. Basically, use in any recipe requiring both garlic and olive oil—which there are many. This will become a staple in your kitchen!

1 large head garlic, peeled

1 pint extra virgin olive oil

In a medium saucepan over medium-low heat, add garlic and oil. Let simmer slowly for 20–30 minutes. Remove from heat and cool to room temperature.

In the meantime, sterilize storage jar in a 275-degree oven for 20 minutes. When olive oil is cool, strain into jar and seal. Oil will last 2–3 months in the refrigerator. Be sure to properly label and date before storing.

Quince Jam

MAKES 5 HALF-PINT (8-OUNCE) JARS

Quince is a fruit that closely resembles a cross between an apple and a pear. Although never eaten raw, when cooked, quince takes on a rosy color and has an alluring aroma, reminiscent of pineapple and guava. Once the cornerstone of most country vegetable gardens, quince is now not as widely available, except in the fall.

Quince is used to make jams, tarts, and preserves, and is a popular ingredient in Middle Eastern cuisine. In Latin countries, it is made into a paste called membrillo, *which is a welcomed addition to cheese and charcuterie platters. The Portuguese word for quince is* marmelo, *which has evolved into the word* marmalade *and is associated with very delicious citrusy fruit preserves.*

5 cups water

6 cups unpeeled grated quince or equal parts Bartlett pears and Golden Delicious apples

1/3 cup fresh-squeezed lemon juice

1 1/2 tablespoons lemon zest

5 cups sugar

Preheat oven to 200 degrees F. Place clean jars on a baking sheet and place in oven for 10 minutes to sterilize. Put seals and rings in a pot of boiling water for 10 minutes; leave in water until ready to cap jars.

Place 5 cups water in a large Dutch oven or heavy-bottom saucepan and bring to a boil over medium heat. Add the quince, lemon juice, and lemon zest. Cook until quince is soft, about 10 minutes. Add sugar, stir to dissolve, and bring to a boil. Lower heat to medium low. Cook, uncovered, stirring occasionally until the jam turns pink and thickens to desired consistency, about 40 minutes. The mixture may seem too liquid, but it will thicken as it ages in the jar.

Using a funnel and ladle, fill sterilized canning jars with the jam—leaving 1/2-inch headspace at the top. Wipe the jar rims clean of any overspill, using a clean damp cloth. Apply the lids and rings and turn jars upside down on a kitchen towel to cool.

Easy Meyer Lemon Marmalade

5 cups water

8 Meyer lemons

5 cups sugar

Marmalade is a jam made with citrus. And because the entire fruit is used, except the seeds, it produces its own pectin, making the addition of commercial pectin unnecessary. Slather it onto your toast, scones, or favorite breads. It can even be used on desserts, meats, and vegetables.

Preheat oven to 225 degrees F. Set clean jars on a baking sheet and place in oven for 10 minutes to sterilize. Put seals and rings in a pot of boiling water for 10 minutes; leave in water until ready to cap jars.

Trim $1/4$-inch off each end of the lemons. Cut each lemon in half and then into quarters. Remove seeds and excess membrane and save. Slice each quarter into thin slices. Combine the seeds, membrane, and ends in a cheesecloth bag or large piece of cheesecloth to form a pectin bag big enough to tie to the pot handle and drop over into the cooking fruit.

In a very large pot over medium heat, add water and bring lemons and pectin bag to a boil. Let boil, uncovered, 30–45 minutes until fruit is soft. If fruit starts to stick to the bottom of pot add a little water. Stir in sugar, lower heat to medium, and boil, stirring occasionally. If foam forms, stir with a wooden spoon to bring the foam back down. Let cook for 20–25 minutes until the temperature, when taken with a candy thermometer, reaches 218–220 degrees. Another way to test is to drop a spoonful on a chilled saucer. If it gels, it is ready.

(continued)

(continued)

Remove marmalade from heat and skim off any foam. Discard the pectin bag. Immediately fill the hot sterilized jars with cooked marmalade. Make sure to stir the marmalade as you go so the fruit remains evenly distributed. Leave a $1/2$-inch headspace in the jars; apply the seals and rings and wipe clean.

For the next step, if you do not have a canning pan with a canning rack insert, use a large Dutch oven or saucepan with a makeshift rack. This can be a small cake cooling rack that will fit inside the pan or a folded kitchen towel. Just make sure the jars do not sit directly on the bottom of the pan.

Heat water in the pan you are using until boiling and totally immerse jars (covered with 1-inch water) for 10 minutes and then remove to a dry kitchen towel. Leave jars undisturbed for at least 12 hours before checking the seals. (You may occasionally hear popping sounds; that is the sound of the jars sealing.) Holding jars at eye level, if the top center of the jar is slightly depressed, the jar is properly sealed—if slightly raised, it is not properly sealed. Sealed jars will store up to 1 year. Unsealed jars should be refrigerated and consumed within a week.

Hot Curried Peaches

This versatile dish works for breakfast or brunch served over pancakes or for dessert atop a big scoop of vanilla ice cream or slice of pound cake. You can even serve it as a side with grilled pork chops or chicken. This recipe can easily be made using canned or frozen peaches if fresh are not available.

Preheat oven to 325 degrees F. Place peaches and cherries in a 9 x 9-inch baking dish.

In a small saucepan over medium-low heat (or in the microwave), melt butter. Remove from heat and stir in sugar, curry powder, spice blend, and salt. Spoon over fruit. Bake 45–60 minutes, or until peaches are soft and syrupy.

This can be made ahead. Reheat in 350-degree oven for 30 minutes.

6 medium peaches, peeled and sliced

1 cup dried cherries or cranberries

5 tablespoons unsalted butter

$\frac{1}{2}$ cup packed light brown sugar

2 teaspoons curry powder

$1\frac{1}{2}$ teaspoons Chef Belinda Moroccan Blend or cinnamon

Pinch of kosher salt

Homemade Sweet and Savory Bourbon Syrup

MAKES APPROXIMATELY 1 CUP

This quick and easy syrup takes only 10 minutes to make. Use it on pancakes, waffles, ice cream, pound cake, and any number of other savory and sweet options. Feel free to substitute vanilla or maple extract for the bourbon, if appropriate for your family. Refrigerate any unused portion and reheat in the microwave before serving.

2 cups packed light brown sugar

1 cup water

1 tablespoon plus 1 teaspoon bourbon

1 teaspoon vanilla or maple extract if substituting for bourbon

In a medium saucepan over medium heat, combine sugar and water. Cook until liquid starts to boil. Reduce heat to medium low and cook for 2 minutes, constantly stirring. Carefully add bourbon. Cook an additional 3 minutes then let cool slightly.

Pour into a sealable jar. Store in a cool dry area or refrigerate. Will last up to 30 days. Syrup will thicken as it cools. Reheat in microwave for 30–40 seconds before serving. Watch closely when reheating to prevent overspill in microwave.

Flavored Butters

Flavored butters provide an extra flavor boost to breads, meats, and sauces.

Honey Butter

1/2 cup unsalted butter, softened

1 tablespoon honey

Pinch of cinnamon

MAKES APPROXIMATELY 1/2 CUP

In a medium bowl, thoroughly combine butter, honey, and cinnamon. Cover and store leftovers in an airtight container and refrigerate for up to 2 months. Butter will last up to 6 months in the freezer.

Strawberry Butter

1/2 cup unsalted butter, softened

6 large strawberries, hulled and chopped

1/4 cup powdered sugar

MAKES APPROXIMATELY 1/2 CUP

In a medium bowl, thoroughly combine butter, strawberries, and sugar. Cover and store leftovers in an airtight container and refrigerate for up to 2 months. Butter will last up to 6 months in the freezer.

Lemon-Herb Butter

1/2 cup unsalted butter, softened

1/2 teaspoon chopped fresh thyme

1/4 teaspoon chopped fresh rosemary

1/2 teaspoon minced garlic

1/2 teaspoon lemon zest

Pinch of kosher salt

MAKES APPROXIMATELY 1/2 CUP

In a medium bowl, thoroughly combine butter, herbs, garlic, zest, and salt. Place butter onto a sheet of parchment paper and roll up into the shape of a log. Twist ends close and refrigerate up to 2 months. Butter will last up to 6 months in the freezer.

Starters

Smoked Salmon Blinis

1 cup all-purpose flour

$3/4$ teaspoon salt

$1/2$ teaspoon baking powder

1 teaspoon superfine sugar

$3/4$ to 1 cup milk

1 large egg

1 tablespoon unsalted butter, melted

1 tablespoon unsalted butter, for cooking (plus additional if needed)

$1/2$ pound smoked salmon

$1/2$ cup Crème Fraîche or sour cream

2 ounces caviar, optional

Fresh dill sprigs

Impress your guests with these easy mini-pancakes—the perfect base for this salmon appetizer. Serve with plenty of the bubbly!

In a medium bowl, combine the flour, salt, baking powder, and sugar. In another bowl, whisk together $3/4$ cup milk, egg, and melted butter. Stir wet ingredients into the flour mixture until just combined, do not overmix. If mixture is still a bit too thick, add additional milk, a few tablespoons at a time, until pouring consistency.

In a large skillet over medium heat, melt 1 tablespoon butter. Using a tablespoon or small scoop, drop batter into skillet and cook until brown, 1–2 minutes per side. Remove to a paper-towel lined platter. Repeat with the remaining batter, adding additional butter to the skillet as necessary.

To assemble, top each blini with a piece of salmon, a dollop of Crème Fraîche, and small amount of caviar. Garnish with dill sprigs.

Crème Fraîche

MAKES 1 CUP

1 cup heavy cream

2 tablespoons buttermilk

Combine cream and buttermilk in a nonreactive container and let sit, covered, at room temperature for 24 hours. Stir, seal, and refrigerate for up to 10 days.

Use in sauces, soups, dips, or as dessert topping.

Country-Style Pâté

MAKES 1 (9 X 5-INCH) LOAF

1 pound ground pork

1/2 pound pepper bacon, chopped or ground in food processor

1/4 cup plain breadcrumbs

1 teaspoon kosher salt

1/2 teaspoon freshly ground black pepper

1/2 tablespoon dried thyme

1/2 teaspoon cardamom

1/2 onion, finely chopped

2 cloves garlic, minced

1/4 cup cognac

1 large egg, lightly beaten

1/4 cup heavy cream

1/2 cup coarsely chopped pistachios or walnuts

Sliced bacon to line loaf pan (about 12 slices)

French bread, thinly sliced, or crostini

Grainy mustard, for serving

Cornichons, for garnish

This is very similar in concept to a delicacy known as souse meat or head cheese made from the leftover scraps of meat from a butchered pig. While many of the original ingredients of souse meat are not as easy to come by, this European cousin is made with ingredients accessible in any supermarket. Spread it on crackers or thinly sliced French bread or crostini with grainy mustard. Pure deliciousness anytime of the day.

Preheat oven to 325 degrees F.

In a large mixing bowl, combine pork, pepper bacon, and breadcrumbs. In a medium bowl, combine salt, pepper, thyme, cardamom, onion, garlic, cognac, egg, cream, and nuts. Stir both mixtures together until well blended. Set aside.

Line a 9 x 5-inch loaf pan with bacon slices. Allow enough bacon to hang over sides to completely cover meat mixture when pan is filled, ensuring ends of loaf pan are also lined. Fill pan with meat mixture and smooth the top; finish covering with the bacon slices. Cover loaf pan tightly with aluminum foil and place in a larger baking pan; transfer to oven. Pour enough boiling water into larger pan to come halfway up sides of loaf pan.

Bake for 2 1/2 hours or until internal temperature reaches 140 degrees F on an instant-read thermometer. Remove from oven and weight with a foil-covered brick or a heavy skillet and cool completely in pan. Refrigerate overnight or up to 4 days.

To unmold, remove foil and place loaf pan in a larger pan of hot water, being careful so the water doesn't get into to the loaf pan, for 5 minutes. Invert onto a platter and wipe away any excess fat. Slice crosswise into $1/2$-inch slices and serve with French bread, mustard, and cornichons. Store leftover pâté in refrigerator up to 10 days, wrapped tightly in plastic wrap.

Spicy Marinated Olives

MAKES 2 CUPS

Serve with appetizers, in salads or cocktails, on charcuterie and cheese trays, or just pop them in your mouth as a snack. You won't be able to stop eating them!

2 cups queen or jumbo olives

1 tablespoon dried thyme

1 tablespoon dried rosemary

1 tablespoon dried oregano

$1/2$ teaspoon crushed red pepper flakes

2 cloves garlic, minced

$1/4$ cup extra virgin olive oil

Put all ingredients in a medium bowl and toss well to coat. Spoon into a glass jar with a tight lid and refrigerate. Olives will keep, refrigerated, for at least 6 months—if they last that long.

Brie, Fig, and Walnut Crostini

SERVES 6 TO 10

Good but not complicated—this is the perfect appetizer for a brunch or party. Substitute goat or blue cheese instead of brie, or make a combination of the three.

Preheat oven to 400 degrees F. Line a baking sheet with aluminum foil.

Place bread slices on baking sheet and brush with olive oil on both sides. Toast in the oven until brown on both sides, about 5 minutes per side.

Spread each crostini with brie, followed with a dollop of fig preserves and sprinkling of walnuts. Arrange on a serving tray and drizzle with honey.

1 French baguette, sliced
  1/2 inch thick diagonally

1/4 cup Garlic-Infused Olive Oil
  (page 23)

1/2 pound wedge brie cheese,
  room temperature

1/2 cup fig preserves

1/2 cup coarsely chopped
  toasted walnuts

Honey, for drizzling

Crab-Stuffed Mushrooms

1 pound medium-size (about 18) mushrooms, stems removed and reserved

2 tablespoons unsalted butter

3 green onions, finely chopped

3 to 4 tablespoons finely chopped red bell pepper

1 large clove garlic, minced

1 cup breadcrumbs

8 ounces crabmeat, picked through to remove shells

1 teaspoon Blackened or Cajun seasoning

1/4 to 1/2 cup white wine

2 tablespoons chopped fresh parsley

Parmesan or pecorino cheese, grated, optional

Prepare these the day before and pop in the oven just before serving. You can easily substitute clams or lobster for the crabmeat. As an entrée, make this recipe with portobello mushrooms, accompanied by a hearty salad.

Preheat oven to 350 degrees F. Prepare a shallow baking dish with nonstick cooking spray.

Using a damp paper towel or clean cloth, wipe the mushrooms and chop the stems. Place mushrooms in baking dish. Melt butter in a large skillet. Add stems, green onions, and bell pepper. Cook until vegetables are tender then add garlic and cook an additional minute. Let cool slightly.

Combine cooked ingredients with breadcrumbs, crabmeat, seasoning, 1/4 cup wine, and parsley. If mixture is still dry, continue adding additional wine until just moist. Evenly spoon or scoop the mixture into mushrooms. Sprinkle each mushroom with cheese, if desired. Bake for 15–20 minutes or until light golden brown and mushrooms are tender.

Tomato Bruschetta

This is a beautiful presentation when using heirloom tomatoes in varying colors. And it is also a quick, easy, and healthy way to use the abundance of tomatoes in your summer garden. You will want to use the best extra virgin olive oil you have on hand.

Preheat oven to 400 degrees F. Line a baking sheet with aluminum foil.

In a medium bowl, combine tomatoes, salt, pepper, basil, and olive oil. Toss to combine and let rest for 10 minutes.

Meanwhile, place bread slices on baking sheet and brush both sides with Garlic-Infused Olive Oil. Toast in the oven until brown on both sides, about 5 minutes per side.

Stir tomato mixture and spoon onto toasted bread slices. Drizzle with leftover infused oil. Arrange on a serving tray.

1 pound heirloom tomatoes (about 3 large tomatoes), seeded and chopped

Kosher salt, to taste

Freshly ground black pepper, to taste

6 fresh basil leaves, stacked, rolled, and cut into ribbons

3 to 4 tablespoons extra virgin olive oil

1 French or Italian baguette, sliced $1/2$ inch thick diagonally

$1/4$ cup Garlic-Infused Olive Oil (page 23)

Bacon Deviled Eggs

SERVES 6

6 hard-boiled eggs

2 tablespoons mayonnaise, more if needed

1 tablespoon Dijon mustard

2 small sweet pickles, chopped, or 2 tablespoons pickle relish

2 slices bacon, cooked crispy and crumbled

Kosher salt, to taste

Freshly ground black pepper, to taste

¼ teaspoon Tabasco sauce

Pinch of curry powder, optional

1 tablespoon chopped fresh parsley

Paprika, for garnish

Chopped fresh chives, for garnish

Deviled eggs have stood the test of time and are a staple at just about every gathering and holiday meal.

Halve eggs and carefully scoop out yolks into a medium bowl. Place whites on a deviled egg serving tray. Using a fork or potato masher, break up yokes into fine smooth pieces. Add mayonnaise, mustard, pickles, half of bacon, salt, pepper, Tabasco, curry powder, and parsley. Place in a piping bag with desired decorative tip, or in a quart-size ziptop bag with 1 corner snipped off, and evenly fill whites. Sprinkle tops of eggs with remaining bacon, paprika, and chives. Refrigerate until ready to serve. Remove 30 minutes before serving.

Coquilles St. Jacques

SERVES 6 AS AN APPETIZER OR 4 AS AN ENTRÉE

This is a seafood and mushroom dish made with a creamy wine sauce baked and served in a scallop shell with a breadcrumb and cheese topping. Traditionally served as an appetizer, it doubles well as an entrée when prepared in larger individual au gratin servers.

Place scallops and shrimp in a medium saucepan with wine and enough clam juice to cover. Add bay leaf, parsley, salt, and pepper. Bring to a simmer and cook slowly for 5 minutes. Drain scallops and shrimp, reserving 1 cup of the liquid. Remove bay leaf and parsley sprigs and discard. Set aside.

In a skillet or sauté pan, melt 2 tablespoons butter and sauté onion, shallots, and mushrooms for about 5 minutes, until soft. Set aside.

In a large saucepan, melt remaining butter and whisk in flour for 2–3 minutes. When the mixture starts to bubble, add the cup of reserved liquid and cream, whisking until well blended and thickened. Add the scallops and shrimp, onions and mushrooms, and crabmeat and stir. Bring to a simmer and adjust seasoning. Remove from heat.

In a medium bowl, combine the breadcrumbs and cheese and set aside.

Preheat broiler. Place 6 baking shells or 4 au gratin dishes on a baking sheet. Fill the shells evenly with the mixture and sprinkle with the breadcrumb mixture. Place under the broiler and broil until the mixture bubbles and the cheese is golden brown. Serve hot.

½ pound bay scallops

½ pound medium shrimp

1 cup dry white wine

Clam juice, as needed

1 bay leaf

3 sprigs parsley

Kosher salt, to taste

Freshly ground black pepper, to taste

5 tablespoons unsalted butter, divided

1 small onion, chopped

2 shallots, sliced

2 cups sliced mushrooms

3 tablespoons all-purpose flour

½ cup heavy cream

½ pound lump crabmeat

1 cup plain breadcrumbs

½ cup grated Gruyère cheese

Endive, Pear, and Goat Cheese Boats

SERVES 15 TO 20

5 Belgian endive, ends trimmed
  and leaves separated

4 ounces spreadable goat or
  blue cheese, or crumbly types
  if preferred

1 large pear (about 8 ounces),
  cored and cut into small
  cubes

1 cup chopped dried figs

1 cup chopped toasted walnuts

Honey, for drizzling

This appetizer requires no cooking. It is easy to prep and pack up in separate containers for quick assembly at your destination if you are taking this to a brunch party. Nothing unhealthy here!

Discard any flawed outer leaves. Spread each leaf with a small amount of cheese on the core end and mound on a small spoonful of chopped pear and figs. At this point, if not serving immediately, place in refrigerator. When ready to serve, sprinkle with a small number of nuts and drizzle with honey.

Jumbo Shrimp and Lump Crab with Vodka Cocktail Sauce

SERVES 6

This ultimate shrimp cocktail is taken to a new level with the addition of lump crab and vodka. What's not to love? Make the sauce a day or two or week ahead. It only gets better with time.

Cocktail Sauce

In a medium bowl, combine the chili sauce, ketchup, horseradish, garlic, celery, lemon juice, Worcestershire sauce, Tabasco, vodka, salt, and black pepper. Refrigerate, covered, until ready to use.

Shrimp

If using raw shrimp, in a medium saucepan on medium-high heat, heat vodka, lemon juice, salt, pepper, shrimp, and enough water to cover shrimp and bring to a boil for 3–5 minutes or until shrimp are pink. Using a slotted spoon, remove shrimp from pan to a bowl and cool thoroughly.

Assembly

Arrange lettuce leaves in bottom of 6 glass ramekins or martini glasses. Divide sauce among glasses and evenly distribute crabmeat in each. Hang 4 shrimp over the sides and garnish with lemon wedges.

Vodka Cocktail Sauce

1/2 cup chili sauce

1 cup ketchup

2 tablespoons horseradish

1 clove garlic, minced

1 stalk celery, finely chopped

1/2 lemon, juiced

1 teaspoon Worcestershire sauce

1 teaspoon Tabasco sauce

2 ounces vodka

Kosher salt and freshly ground
  black pepper, to taste

Poached Shrimp

1/2 cup vodka

1/2 lemon, juiced

Kosher salt and freshly ground
  black pepper, to taste

24 raw jumbo/colossal shrimp,
  peeled and deveined with
  tails on, or ready-to-use
  cooked shrimp

Bibb or Boston whole lettuce
  leaves, optional

1 pound lump crabmeat, picked
  over for shells and divided

Lemon wedges, for garnish

Avocado Toast Points

4 slices pumpernickel or whole-grain bread, toasted

2 ripe avocados, halved and sliced

Kosher salt, to taste

Freshly ground black pepper, to taste

Pinch of crushed red pepper

Fresh-squeezed lemon juice

Extra virgin olive oil, optional

1 large Roma tomato, cut into 8 thin slices

Alfalfa sprouts or micro greens, to taste

It doesn't get any easier than this—a heart-healthy brunch snack in less than five minutes. Don't forget the mimosa!

Top each slice of toast with a half avocado. Using the back of a fork, mash and spread over entire slice. Sprinkle with salt, pepper, and crushed red pepper. Squeeze on a small amount of lemon juice and drizzle with olive oil. Cut toast in half diagonally. Top with a tomato slice and sprouts.

Cheesy Grit Cakes

MAKES APPROXIMATELY 20 CAKES

These little cakes serve as the perfect base for your favorite appetizer or meat topping.

In a large pot over medium heat, bring milk to a boil and add salt. Gradually stir in grits and reduce heat to low. Simmer, stirring frequently, until grits are thick and creamy, adding more milk if necessary, about 45 minutes. Remove from heat and stir in cheese, butter, pepper, cayenne, and chives until cheese is melted.

Spread grits in an even layer onto a 9 x 13-inch parchment-lined baking sheet, and let cool completely. Cover with plastic wrap and refrigerate until firm. Using a 2-inch square cookie cutter, cut out cakes and refrigerate until ready to serve.

When ready to serve, transfer cakes to a parchment or foil-lined baking sheet and place under broiler for 5–7 minutes until lightly golden brown. Add toppings of choice.

4 cups milk or chicken stock

Kosher salt, to taste

1 cup stone-ground grits

1/2 cup grated cheddar cheese

2 tablespoons unsalted butter

Freshly ground black pepper, to taste

1/4 teaspoon cayenne pepper

2 tablespoons chopped fresh chives

Caramelized Onions and Feta Mini Tarts

MAKES 36

1 to 2 tablespoons olive oil

2 large red onions, chopped

2 teaspoon fresh thyme leaves, chopped

4 (9-inch) pie crust dough, homemade or store-bought

1 cup crumbled feta cheese, optional

1/4 cup sliced Kalamata olives or chopped roasted red bell peppers

3 large eggs

3/4 cup heavy cream

Kosher salt, to taste

White pepper, to taste

This is a wonderfully easy and delicious appetizer for brunch, a cocktail party, or a snack, and is the ultimate finger food. Make them the day ahead or earlier on the same day as served. Reheat in microwave or serve at room temperature.

Preheat oven to 350 degrees F.

Heat 1 tablespoon oil in a nonstick skillet over medium-low heat. Add onions and cook until caramelized, about 20 minutes, stirring occasionally; adding additional oil as needed. Stir in thyme, remove from heat, and set aside to cool.

Grease a 24-cup and a 12-cup mini muffin pan. Roll out dough, and using a 3-inch round cookie or biscuit cutter, cut dough into 36 rounds (9 from each sheet of dough) and line the cups of the muffin pans.

Put 1/2 teaspoon of the onion mixture in each of the 36 cups and then 1/2 teaspoon of feta. Add a slice of olive on top if using. In a 2-cup measuring bowl with a spout, whisk eggs, cream, salt, and pepper; pour equal portions into each tartlet shell, just enough to cover ingredients, but not overflow. Bake 20–25 minutes or until puffed and light golden in color. Remove from oven and allow to cool in pan for 5 minutes. Transfer to a wire rack and cool completely.

If made ahead, place in a sealed plastic container or bag and refrigerate.

Egg
Dishes

Spinach and Goat Cheese Eggs Florentine with Hollandaise Sauce

SERVES 4

This breakfast classic is a lot easier to prepare than you think. With a few simple steps to master, like poaching the eggs and using a blender to make the hollandaise sauce, this will become one of your new favorites.

In a large skillet or sauté pan, heat oil over medium heat. Sauté shallot until soft, 2–3 minutes; add spinach and cook until slightly wilted, 1–2 minutes. Add balsamic vinegar and cook, stirring constantly, until most of vinegar has evaporated, about 1 minute. Season with salt and pepper. Set aside and keep warm.

Break each egg into a separate small prep bowl. (This decreases the chances of damaging the eggs as you introduce them to the simmering water.) In a deep nonstick skillet, add about 2 inches of water and bring to a boil then reduce to simmer. Add distilled vinegar. Slide each egg into the simmering water—clockwise, so you can keep track of how long each egg cooks. Cover and cook approximately 4 minutes, until whites are set but not hard. Remove eggs with a slotted spoon, in order, and drain on a paper towel.

To assemble, place a piece of toast on each serving plate. Follow with equal amounts of the spinach mixture, goat cheese, and a poached egg then drizzle with Easy Hollandaise Sauce. Garnish with chives.

(continued)

1 tablespoon olive oil

1 shallot, thinly sliced

1 pound baby spinach, kale, or arugula

1 tablespoon balsamic vinegar

Kosher salt, to taste

Freshly ground black pepper, to taste

4 large very fresh whole eggs

1 tablespoon white distilled vinegar

4 slices thick sourdough bread, toasted

Goat cheese, crumbled

Easy Hollandaise Sauce (page 55)

Chopped fresh chives

(continued)

Easy Hollandaise Sauce

MAKES ⅓ CUP

For best results, make sauce just before serving.

1 large egg yolk

1½ teaspoons fresh-squeezed lemon juice

Pinch of cayenne pepper

4 tablespoons unsalted butter, melted and warm

Kosher salt, to taste

Into the bowl of a blender, add egg yolk, lemon juice, and cayenne. Pulse a few times to combine. Drizzle the butter into the running blender until egg mixture becomes smooth and frothy. If sauce is too thick, add a teaspoon of lukewarm water. Add salt and serve. If not serving immediately keep warm in a heatproof bowl over hot water.

Mushroom, Ham, and Bell Pepper Omelet

MAKES 1 OMELET

3 large eggs, room temperature

1 tablespoon heavy cream or half-and-half

Kosher salt, to taste

Freshly ground black pepper, to taste

Dash of Tabasco or hot sauce

1 teaspoon freshly chopped herbs such as thyme, chives, or tarragon, divided

2 tablespoon unsalted butter

1/2 cup sliced mushrooms

1/4 cup chopped ham

1/4 cup sliced roasted red bell peppers

Grated Swiss or Gruyère cheese, to taste

What would brunch be without an omelet? Fill it with anything your heart desires and then some. There is no right or wrong way to eat them.

In a small bowl, whisk together eggs, cream, salt, pepper, Tabasco, and 1/2 teaspoon herbs until combined.

In an 8-inch nonstick omelet pan over medium heat, melt butter. Sauté mushrooms until most of liquid is evaporated. Add ham and bell pepper and continue sautéing until mushrooms are soft and brown. Add egg mixture and lower temperature to medium-low. Let eggs cook about 30 seconds until starting to set. With a heat-resistant spatula, lift sides of omelet and tilt skillet to let uncooked eggs run under the omelet—do this all the way around the omelet until it is set (no longer runny).

Spread cheese over half of the omelet. Using the spatula, fold the side without cheese onto the cheese half. Carefully slide omelet onto a plate and serve. Garnish with remaining herbs.

Loaded Steak and Bell Pepper Strata

SERVES 4 TO 6

A strata is an egg and milk custard pie with main ingredients consisting of bread, cheese, and eggs, but can also include other supporting ingredients such as meats and vegetables. This dish is ideally made the day ahead and refrigerated to allow the bread to absorb the egg mixture. Remove from refrigerator 30 minutes before baking.

Butter an 8 x 8-inch baking dish. Place bread cubes into dish. Layer with cheese, bell pepper, broccoli, onion, and steak.

In a medium bowl, whisk together eggs, milk, salt, pepper, nutmeg, cayenne, and parsley. Pour custard over bread. Wrap with plastic wrap and refrigerate overnight. Remove from refrigerator 30 minutes before baking. Remove plastic wrap.

Preheat oven to 350 degrees F. Bake until cheese is melted and the custard is set in the center, about 45 minutes. Let cool slightly and serve warm.

1 tablespoon butter

2 cups cubed day-old bread

1 cup grated Gruyère or fontina cheese

1 large red bell pepper, trimmed, seeded, and sliced

1 cup broccoli florets

1/2 red onion, sliced

1/2 pound leftover cooked steak or pot roast, thinly sliced

4 large eggs

1 1/2 cups milk

Kosher salt, to taste

White pepper, to taste

1/4 teaspoon nutmeg

Pinch of cayenne pepper

1 tablespoon chopped fresh parsley

Fluffy Scrambled Eggs on Texas Toast with Swiss Cheese

SERVES 2

1 tablespoon unsalted butter

4 large eggs

2 tablespoons heavy cream or half-and-half

Kosher salt, to taste

1 scallion or green onion (white and light green parts), chopped

2 slices Texas toast

2 to 4 slices Swiss cheese (depending on size of bread)

1 avocado, halved and sliced, optional

1 large beefsteak tomato, sliced

Freshly ground black pepper

This should fill the hunger gap for the vegetarians in your group. Just add fruit. Texas toast can generally be found in supermarkets, but you can easily make it at home if you have access to whole artisan bread.

In a medium skillet over medium heat, melt butter. In a small bowl, add eggs, cream, and salt. Whisk vigorously until yolks and whites are thoroughly combined—eggs will be slightly lighter in color.

Add eggs to skillet and lower heat to medium low. Using a rubber spatula, gently push eggs from one side of skillet to the other, scooping and turning as you go. Continue until eggs get fluffy and form large curds. While eggs are still wet, fold in scallions and remove pan from heat. Note that eggs will continue to cook in pan from the residual heat.

To assemble, place a piece of toast on each serving plate. Follow with cheese slices, avocado slices, and tomato slices then top with eggs. Finish with freshly cracked pepper and garnish with additional scallions, if desired.

Texas Toast

1 tablespoon Garlic-Infused Olive Oil (page 23)

1 tablespoon unsalted butter, melted

2 (1-inch) slices whole-loaf artisan bread

MAKES 2 SLICES TOAST

Preheat a cast iron skillet on medium heat. Combine oil and butter and spread on both sides of bread slices. Fry bread until brown on both sides.

Italian Baked Eggs and Sausage in Marinara Sauce

SERVES 4

This is an easy one-pan meal that is great for breakfast, lunch, or dinner and goes from oven to table in less than 30 minutes!

Preheat oven to 400 degrees F.

Heat oil in a cast iron or ovenproof skillet over medium heat. Crumble sausage in skillet and cook, stirring, until brown. Make a well in center of sausage and add onion; sauté until soft. Add garlic and cook an additional minute. Stir until meat, onion, and garlic are well combined. Stir in marinara, pepper flakes, and half of basil and bring to a simmer.

Top evenly with mozzarella and Parmesan cheeses. Make 4 dents in sauce and crack an egg into each dent, leaving space between each egg. Season eggs with salt and pepper. Transfer skillet to oven and bake 15 minutes or until eggs are desired consistency. Remove from oven and garnish with remaining basil and additional Parmesan. Serve with lots of crusty bread.

1 tablespoon olive oil

1 pound bulk Italian sausage, or links removed from casing

1 small onion, chopped

1 clove garlic, minced

4 cups marinara sauce, store-bought or homemade

Pinch of red pepper flakes

1 tablespoon chopped fresh basil, divided

1/2 cup grated mozzarella cheese

1/4 cup freshly grated Parmesan cheese

4 large eggs, room temperature

Kosher salt, to taste

Freshly ground black pepper, to taste

Salmon-Asparagus Quiche

SERVES 8 AS A MAIN COURSE

OR 12 AS AN APPETIZER

1 (9-inch) pie crust

12 to 16 asparagus spears, tough ends trimmed

1 tablespoon unsalted butter

$1/2$ medium onion, sliced

3 large eggs

1 cup heavy cream or half-and-half

Kosher salt, to taste

White pepper, to taste

1 teaspoon chopped fresh dill

$1/4$ teaspoon grated fresh nutmeg, optional

$1^1/2$ cups grated Gruyère cheese

4 ounces sliced smoked salmon

Want to show those you care about how special they really are? Say it with this quiche. Oh, and don't forget the champagne!

Preheat oven to 375 degrees F. Place pie crust into a 9-inch quiche pan or pie plate. Trim off any hangover if necessary. Cover pie crust surface and sides with parchment or wax paper and weight with pie weights or raw beans. (If using a traditional quiche pan with a removable bottom, place pan on a rimmed baking sheet.) Blind-bake* crust for 8–10 minutes. Remove from oven and set aside to cool before filling.

Bring a large pot of salted water to a boil. Blanch the asparagus spears for 2–3 minutes; remove and immediately shock in an ice water bath. Drain, pat dry, and set aside.

Melt butter in a medium skillet over medium heat, and sauté onion until soft. In a medium bowl, whisk eggs, cream, salt, pepper, dill, and nutmeg.

To assemble: Sprinkle half of cheese in the bottom of crust and cover with onion. Next, evenly layer salmon slices, followed by asparagus spears arranged like spokes of a wheel. Sprinkle on the remainder of cheese and cover with the egg mixture. Let rest for 15 minutes so egg custard can settle into the other ingredients. Bake for 40–45 minutes until set.

*Blind-baking a pie crust is baking it without the filling. The reason to do this is to ensure that once the pie crust is filled and baked, that it does not become soggy or fall apart under the weight of the filling.

Spinach-Chorizo Frittata

SERVES 8 TO 12

Frittatas are an easy entertaining option—make them with whatever ingredients you have on hand. And with no crust to make, you can have it on the table in very little time.

Preheat oven to 350 degrees F.

Heat olive oil in a large cast iron or ovenproof skillet over medium heat. Add chorizo and onion and cook until chorizo is brown and onion is translucent. Remove from heat and let cool slightly. In another nonstick skillet over medium heat, wilt the spinach then spread out on a baking sheet to cool. Squeeze all excess water out of spinach and spread over the sausage mixture.

In a medium bowl, whisk together eggs, cream, salt, pepper, oregano, and tomatoes. Pour into the skillet over the sausage mixture. Cover evenly with cheese. Put skillet back on stovetop over medium heat and cook, scrambling lightly, until eggs start to set, 5–7 minutes. Place in oven and cook until completely set, the center should not move when pan is shaken, 20–25 minutes. Let cool for 10 minutes before slicing and serving. Garnish with cilantro.

1 tablespoon extra virgin olive oil

1/2 pound chorizo, cut into small dice

1 medium onion, diced

1/2 pound fresh spinach, washed and drained

10 large eggs

1/2 cup heavy cream or half-and-half

Kosher salt, to taste

Freshly ground black pepper, to taste

1 teaspoon dried oregano

2 tablespoons thinly sliced sun-dried tomatoes

1 cup grated cheddar cheese

Chopped cilantro, for garnish

Sausage, Cheddar, and Polenta Soufflé

SERVES 4

Unsalted butter

All-purpose flour

1 tablespoon olive oil

1/2 pound bulk Italian sausage

2 tablespoons chopped
  scallions

11/2 cups milk

Kosher salt, to taste

1/2 cup polenta, coarse
  cornmeal, or grits

Freshly ground black pepper,
  to taste

Pinch of cayenne pepper

1/2 cup grated sharp cheddar
  cheese

4 large eggs

1/4 teaspoon cream of tartar

This sausage-filled soufflé is almost like a light and fluffy version of an oven-baked omelet. Make it with whatever corn grain you have on hand—polenta, cornmeal, or grits.

Preheat oven to 350 degrees F. Butter and flour 4 (1-cup) ramekins.

Heat olive oil in a medium skillet over medium heat. Cook sausage until brown then add scallions and continue to cook until soft. Set aside.

In a medium pot over medium heat, bring milk to a boil. Gradually stir in polenta, salt, pepper, and cayenne and whisk 2–4 minutes or until thickened. Remove from heat and stir in cheese. Let cool slightly.

Into 2 bowls, separate egg yolks and whites. Whisk egg yolks into cooled polenta. In a large bowl using a hand mixer, beat egg whites and cream of tartar until stiff. Gently fold half of the egg whites into the polenta mixture, and then fold in the rest.

Divide the sausage mixture into the ramekins and fill with the egg mixture. Bake 20–25 minutes until slightly brown and firm. Soufflés are best served right out of the oven.

Soups, Salads & Sandwiches

Fiery Stout Chili

SERVES 10 TO 15

I just had to include this recipe for the all of the football junkies who "tailgate" brunch on Sundays! Beware, this chili packs a lot of heat. You may want to step down a notch on the Scoville scale of chile peppers used in this recipe.

4 tablespoons canola or vegetable oil, divided

4 to 5 slices thick bacon, cut into 1/2-inch pieces

2 red bell peppers, diced

2 jalapeños or serrano peppers, minced, plus extra

6 poblano chiles, roasted*, peeled and chopped

2 yellow onions, chopped

6 to 8 cloves garlic, minced

1 pound boneless chuck, trimmed and cut into 1/4-inch cubes

2 pounds coarsely ground beef

1 pound medium or hot bulk Italian sausage

4 tablespoons all-purpose seasoning

3 tablespoons chili powder

2 teaspoons ground cumin

2 cups tomato sauce

1 cup tomato paste

1 (12-ounce) bottle Guinness Stout (lager or pale ale is acceptable)

1 cup beef stock

2 (15.5-ounce) cans pinto or chili beans, with liquid

2 (15.5-ounce) cans black beans, with liquid

1 bunch scallions, thinly sliced diagonally

1 to 2 cups shredded sharp cheddar cheese

Heat 2 tablespoons oil in a large stock pot over medium-high heat. Cook bacon pieces until starting to brown. Add bell peppers, jalapeños, chiles, and onions and cook until tender, about 7 minutes. Add garlic and cook 1 minute longer.

In another large skillet or Dutch oven, heat remaining oil over medium-high heat. Add chuck and brown. Crumble ground beef and sausage, trying not to break up ground beef too much, and cook until nicely brown and cooked through, 7–10 minutes. Pour and stir meat mixture into stock pot with vegetables. Add seasoning, chili powder, and cumin and cook for 1 minute. Add tomato sauce and paste and stir for 2 minutes. Stir in beer and stock. Lower heat, cover, and simmer for 2 hours. Add beans 30 minutes before end of cooking time. Serve in bowls and garnish with scallions, cheese, and sliced jalapeños.

*To Roast Peppers: Slice peppers in half and remove seeds and core. Lay, skin side up, on a foil- or parchment-lined baking sheet. Place pan 4–6 inches under the oven broiler for 5–10 minutes, until they blacken and blister. Remove from oven and seal in a ziplock bag for 30–60 minutes. Peel off and discard the blistered skin.

Roasted Butternut Squash Soup with Scallops

MAKES 8 CUPS OR 5 BOWLS

This soup is a refreshing starter to any meal—or as a meal itself. Just add a salad.

Soup

Preheat oven to 350 degrees F. Spray a 9 x 13-inch glass baking dish with nonstick cooking spray. Cut squash in half lengthwise and place, cut side down, in prepared baking dish. Bake until squash is tender, about 45–60 minutes.

Heat oil in a deep medium-size skillet or small Dutch oven over medium heat. Sauté onion until soft, about 5 minutes. Add garlic and cook for 1 more minute.

Using a large spoon, scrape half squash from skin into a blender; add half of onion mixture and purée until smooth. Transfer to a clean pot and keep warm and covered. Repeat with second half of squash and onion mixture and add to pot. Stir in broth, cardamom, and Madeira and bring to a simmer. Season with salt and pepper and continue to simmer, uncovered, until thickened, about 15 minutes. Remove from heat, cover, and keep warm.

Crostini

Preheat oven to 400 degrees F.

Slice a baguette into 1/2-inch slices. Brush with olive oil then sprinkle lightly with garlic and parsley. Place on a baking sheet and bake for 8–10 minutes, turning once, until slightly brown around the edges.

(continued)

Soup

1 butternut squash (3 to 4 pounds)

Extra virgin olive oil

1/2 large onion, peeled and sliced

2 cloves garlic, minced

3 cups chicken broth, more if needed

1/2 teaspoon cardamom

2 tablespoons Madeira or sherry

Kosher salt, to taste

Freshly ground black pepper, to taste

Crostini

1 baguette

Extra virgin olive oil, to taste

Granulated garlic, to taste

Minced parsley, to taste

(continued)

Scallops

8 sea scallops

Grains of paradise, to taste

Extra virgin olive oil

Scallops

Sprinkle scallops with grains of paradise and chill for 30 minutes. Heat oil in a skillet over medium-high heat until hot. Sauté scallops until just cooked through, 2–3 minutes per side. Transfer to a paper towel.

Spoon warm soup into individual bowls. Add a crostini and top with a scallop.

Avocado BLT

SERVES 4

8 slices sourdough bread, toasted

4 leaves crispy lettuce (romaine, iceberg, green leaf)

2 avocados, pitted and sliced

1 large tomato, sliced thinly into 8 slices

8 slices thick bacon, cooked crispy and halved

2 tablespoons mayonnaise

This is a time-tested and honored sandwich, with a twist, that just won't go away. The avocado puts a healthy spin on this sandwich without changing why you fell in love with it in the first place. Feel free to use sliced turkey instead of the bacon.

Lay 4 slices of toast on a clean flat surface. Top each with 1 lettuce leaf, $1/2$ avocado, 2 slices bacon, and 2 slices tomato. On 1 side of the remaining bread slices, spread with mayonnaise, and place on top of sandwich. Cut in half diagonally and serve.

Seafood Chowder

SERVES 8

The beauty of this recipe is that you can substitute any seafood or fish that is readily available wherever you live. Experiment and enjoy!

Heat olive oil in a large stock pot, saucepan, or Dutch oven. Sauté the bacon pieces until crispy. Remove to a paper towel-lined platter. Add the onion and sauté until translucent. Whisk in the flour to make a roux. Cook over medium heat for about 5 minutes. Do not allow to brown. Gradually whisk in the clam juice, blending until smooth and thickened. Heat to a boil. Reduce to a simmer. Add the potatoes and carrots and simmer gently.

When potatoes and carrots are three-fourths cooked, 5–6 minutes, add the shrimp, scallops, clams, crabmeat, and bacon and cook another 10 minutes.

Temper the heavy cream into the soup by mixing with 1 cup of the hot soup mixture and stirring vigorously back into the pot. Add wine and seafood spice blend. Serve with crusty bread.

4 tablespoons olive oil

4 slices bacon, cut into 1/4-inch pieces

1 small onion, chopped

1/2 cup all-purpose flour

1 1/2 quarts clam juice

2 medium potatoes, diced

2 medium carrots, thick sliced and halved

1/2 pound shrimp

1/2 pound bay scallops, halved

1 (10-ounce) can clams, drained

1/2 pound lump crabmeat

8 ounces heavy cream

1/2 cup white wine

1 teaspoon seafood spice blend

Parsley, for garnish

Simple Butter Lettuce Salad

SERVES 8

¼ cup white wine vinegar

⅓ cup Garlic-Infused Olive Oil (page 23)

1 teaspoon Dijon mustard

Kosher salt, to taste

Freshly ground black pepper, to taste

2 heads butter, Boston, or Bibb lettuce

1 cup packed arugula

This is the perfect salad for feeding a large crowd. It provides that transitional phase of the meal and cleanses the palate without ruining the appetite for the rest of the meal that follows.

In the bottom of a large salad bowl, whisk together vinegar, oil, mustard, salt, and pepper.

Pull lettuce leaves apart, leaving smaller leaves whole and tearing larger leaves in half. Place lettuce and arugula in salad bowl on top of dressing and toss.

If not serving immediately, refrigerate without tossing. When ready to serve, remove from refrigerator and toss.

Creamy Tomato Soup with Crostini Cheese Toast

SERVES 4

A new take on an old tried-and-true favorite. Tomato soup and grilled cheese will never go away—it just keeps getting reinvented and better.

Soup

In a large saucepan, heat oil over medium heat. Sauté onion, carrot, and celery until onion is translucent. Add garlic and cook an additional minute. Stir in tomato paste and continue to cook until it starts to caramelize, 4–5 minutes.

Add stock, tomatoes, 1 teaspoon sugar, and thyme sprigs. Increase heat to medium high and bring to a boil. Reduce heat to medium-low, cover, and simmer until soup reduces and thickens, about 45 minutes. Remove from heat and let cool slightly. Discard the thyme sprigs. Working in batches, purée soup in a blender until smooth. Add puréed soup batches to a clean pot. Stir in cream and simmer soup an additional 10–15 minutes. Season to taste with salt and pepper, adding remaining teaspoon of sugar if needed.

Crostini Cheese Toast

Preheat oven to 375 degrees F. Brush bread slices on both sides with olive oil and place on a baking sheet. Bake 5–7 minutes on each side until crisp and edges are starting to turn brown. Sprinkle crostini with equal amounts of each cheese, return to oven, and bake until cheese melts.

Ladle soup into individual bowls or mugs; garnish with fresh thyme and serve with cheese toast.

Soup

- 2 tablespoons extra virgin olive oil
- 1 large onion, diced
- 1 carrot, diced
- 1 stalk celery, diced
- 2 cloves garlic, sliced
- 2 tablespoons tomato paste
- 3 cups unsalted chicken or vegetable stock
- 1 (28-ounce) can whole peeled plum tomatoes, including juice
- 1 to 2 teaspoons sugar
- 3 to 4 sprigs fresh thyme
- 1/3 cup heavy cream
- Kosher salt, to taste
- Freshly ground black pepper, to taste
- Fresh thyme, for garnish

Crostini Cheese Toast

- 8 thick slices of baguette or artisan loaf
- Extra virgin olive oil
- 1/2 cup grated Gruyère cheese
- 1/2 cup grated sharp cheddar cheese

Crab Louie Salad

SERVES 6 TO 8

The elegance of this salad makes it ideally suited to the fanciest brunch. Serve it as the main course during the warmer months or as a side for more elaborate brunches. Traditionally this salad is made with Dungeness crab, but use whatever fresh crab is in season and available in your area.

Dressing

1½ cups mayonnaise

¼ cup ketchup

¼ cup chili sauce

1 teaspoon prepared horseradish

1 tablespoon fresh-squeezed lemon juice

1 tablespoon sweet pickle relish

1 tablespoon finely chopped sweet onion

½ teaspoon Worcestershire sauce

Kosher salt, to taste

Freshly ground black pepper, to taste

1 tablespoon finely chopped parsley

Salad

1 pound thin asparagus, trimmed

1 romaine heart, cut crosswise ½-inch thick

1 head iceberg, chopped

½ English cucumber, halved and sliced

4 radishes, thinly sliced

2 avocados, pitted and sliced

2 heirloom tomatoes, cut into wedges

2 hard-boiled eggs, cut into wedges

1 pound crabmeat

1 lemon, cut into wedges

Dressing

In a medium bowl, whisk together mayonnaise, ketchup, chili sauce, horseradish, lemon juice, relish, onion, Worcestershire sauce, salt, pepper, and parsley. Make the day before and refrigerate. Bring to room temperature before dressing salad.

Salad

Bring salted water to a boil in a pan or deep skillet. Cook asparagus for 3–4 minutes until tender, but still firm. Drain and cool. Set aside.

Arrange the lettuces, cucumber, radishes, avocados, tomatoes, asparagus, and eggs on a large serving platter. Top with the crabmeat and garnish with lemon wedges. Serve dressing on the side or pass at the table.

Sausage, Lentil, and Bacon Soup

SERVES 8

This hearty soup, which includes sausage and bacon, is more like a stew. Served with lots of crusty bread, it is a standalone meal on a cold or rainy day. Make lots and freeze for future meals. This soup will last up to six months in the freezer.

In a large stock pot over medium heat, cook bacon until crisp. Remove from pot using a slotted spoon and drain on a paper towel. Cook the sausage until cooked through and brown, 5–7 minutes. Remove from pot and keep warm.

Add olive oil to the same pot and sauté the onion, carrots, and celery until the onion is soft, 3–4 minutes. Add garlic and cook an additional minute. Add lentils, stock, thyme, oregano, salt, pepper, bay leaves, pepper flakes, and meats to the pot and bring to a boil. Lower heat and simmer, stirring occasionally, for 45–60 minutes or until lentils are soft. Remove bay leaves and discard. Ladle into bowls and garnish with parsley and cheese.

6 to 8 slices bacon, cut crosswise into 1/2-inch pieces

1 pound Italian sausage (bulk or links) removed from casing and crumbled

2 tablespoons olive oil

1 large yellow onion, diced

2 carrots, halved and sliced diagonally

2 celery stalks, sliced diagonally

3 to 4 cloves garlic, minced

16 ounces lentils, sorted and rinsed

8 cups unsalted chicken stock

1 teaspoon dried thyme

1 teaspoon dried oregano

Kosher salt, to taste

Freshly ground black pepper, to taste

2 bay leaves

Pinch of red pepper flakes

Chopped parsley, for garnish

Grated Romano or Parmesan cheese, for garnish

Egg, Prosciutto, Tomato, and Arugula Panini

SERVES 4

2 to 3 tablespoons Garlic-Infused Olive Oil (page 23)

8 thick slices ciabatta or other rustic bread

8 slices fontina cheese

6 large eggs, scrambled

8 slices prosciutto

1 large tomato, sliced thinly into 8 slices

1 cup packed arugula (about 2 ounces)

No panini press—no problem! These sandwiches can just as easily be prepared in a cast iron skillet or grill pan. All that is needed is a press, which can be another skillet, to serve as a weight during cooking.

Lay bread slices on a clean flat surface, like a large cutting board. Brush 1 side of each slice with olive oil and turn that side down. On the unoiled side of 4 slices, place 1 slice of cheese, $1/4$ of eggs, 2 slices of prosciutto, 2 tomato slices, arugula, another cheese slice, and top with remaining bread slices, unoiled side next to the arugula.

Heat panini press according to manufacturer's instructions. Working 2 sandwiches at a time, or 1, depending on the size of the press, place sandwiches on panini press and pull the top down. Cook until browned, 5–7 minutes. Repeat with remaining sandwiches. Remove from press, cut in half, and serve.

Grit Cake, Collard, and Pulled Pork Sammie

MAKES 15–20 DEPENDING ON SIZE OF CAKES

Cabbage collards are a variety of collard greens that are well-known and grown in the Carolinas, but are only now spreading to other states. They are more tender and milder than the regular collards and cook in almost half the time. This recipe is prepared intentionally without bacon, or other smoked meats, because the greens will be paired with pulled pork. This open-face sammie is like a party in your mouth.

Strip greens from the stems and rinse thoroughly to remove dirt and sand. Working a few leaves at a time, stack leaves on top of each other, roll up, and cut into 1/2-inch slices. Set aside.

Heat oil in a Dutch oven over medium-low heat. Cook garlic slowly, to extract the flavor but not brown, 2–3 minutes. Gradually add greens to pan, a handful at a time. They will cook down quickly. Stir to mix with the garlic. Add stock, sugar, and crushed pepper. Simmer until tender, about 45 minutes. Add salt and vinegar. Keep warm.

When making the grit cakes, you will want to cut them slightly bigger in size. On a large serving tray or on individual plates, arrange cakes, top with a scoop of pulled pork and flatten the top slightly. Add a small scoop of greens. Serve with barbecue sauce on the side.

2 bunches cabbage collard greens

1 to 2 tablespoons vegetable oil

1 tablespoon minced garlic

2 to 3 cups unsalted chicken or vegetable stock

1 tablespoon sugar

1/4 teaspoon crushed red pepper

Kosher salt, to taste

1 tablespoon apple cider vinegar

Cheesy Grit Cakes (page 49)

Oven-Roasted Pulled Pork (page 126)

Barbecue sauce, for serving

Croque Madame

5 tablespoons unsalted butter, divided

2 tablespoons all-purpose flour

1 cup milk, room temperature

Kosher salt, to taste

White pepper, to taste

Pinch of nutmeg

1½ cups grated Gruyère cheese

8 thick slices brioche

4 teaspoons Dijon mustard

12 slices deli ham

4 large eggs

Freshly ground black pepper, to taste

A croque madame is a hot ham and cheese sandwich topped with a fried egg. Without the egg, it is referred to as croque monsieur. Both of these sandwiches are served warm, dripping with a Gruyère cheese sauce. This sandwich is the perfect choice for a light brunch.

Preheat broiler. In a medium saucepan over medium-low heat, melt 2 tablespoons butter. Whisk in flour and cook, stirring constantly, 2–3 minutes. Gradually add milk while whisking and continue whisking until mixture starts to thicken. Reduce heat and let simmer, whisking occasionally, for 4–5 minutes. Remove from heat and stir in salt, white pepper, nutmeg, and half the cheese. Set aside and let cool slightly.

Spray a baking sheet or shallow baking pan with nonstick cooking spray and set aside. Spread 4 slices of brioche with mustard and top each with 3 slices of ham. Spread top of ham with some of the sauce and top with another slice of bread.

In a large skillet, add remaining butter. When hot, brown 2 sandwiches on both sides, about 2 minutes per side. Place sandwiches on baking sheet and repeat with remaining 2 sandwiches. Brush the top of sandwiches with the remaining sauce and sprinkle with the remaining cheese.

Using the same skillet, wipe out and spray with nonstick cooking spray. Over medium-low heat, gently crack the eggs into the pan, without breaking the yolks. Season with salt and black pepper. Cook until whites are set and yolk is runny, about 3 minutes. Meanwhile place sandwiches under the broiler and broil for 2–3 minutes until sauce is bubbly and golden brown. Top each sandwich with an egg and serve immediately.

Egg, Bacon, and Cheese Brunch Burger

SERVES 4

Who doesn't love a good burger? Breakfast, lunch, or dinner, brunch is the perfect time to indulge in our favorite sandwich.

In a skillet or saucepan over medium heat, melt 1 tablespoon butter. Add onion and salt, toss, and cook for 25–30 minutes, stirring only occasionally. Stirring too often will prevent the onion from browning and caramelizing. Let cook until brown in color. Set aside.

Preheat oven to 350 degrees F.

In a large bowl, combine chuck, salt, pepper, garlic, and chives. Mix well and shape into 4 equal-size patties. In a large skillet over medium heat, melt remaining butter. If using a grill pan, spray with cooking spray. Cook patties for 4–5 minutes on each side or to your preferred doneness. Top each with a slice of cheese and transfer to oven to melt, about 3 minutes. Remove and keep warm. At this time cook eggs according to your preference.

To build burger, place muffin bottoms on a clean flat surface. On each, add a lettuce leaf, tomato slice, 2 pickle slices, burger with melted cheese, caramelized onions, 1 whole slice of bacon torn in half, and an egg. Finish with top muffin. Serve with your choice of condiments.

2 tablespoons unsalted butter, divided

1/2 red onion, sliced into half moons

Pinch of kosher salt

1 1/2 pounds ground chuck

Kosher salt, to taste

Freshly ground black pepper, to taste

2 cloves garlic, minced

2 teaspoons finely chopped chives

4 slices Gruyère or Gouda cheese

4 large eggs, fried or poached

4 English muffins, toasted (or your favorite bun)

4 lettuce leaves

1 large tomato, sliced

8 slices sandwich pickles

4 slices thick bacon, fried crispy

Condiments, of choice

Spicy Egg and Chicken Wraps

SERVES 8

2 boneless, skinless chicken breasts, cut into ¼-inch strips

Kosher salt, to taste

Freshly ground black pepper, to taste

2 teaspoons chipotle chile powder

2 tablespoons vegetable oil

4 tablespoons unsalted butter

3 large poblano chile peppers, seeded and diced

8 scallions, chopped

½ cup chopped cilantro, divided

8 large eggs, beaten

1 cup crumbled queso fresco or Monterey Jack cheese

8 (10-inch) flour tortillas, warmed

¾ cup spicy salsa, optional

Wraps make for a wonderful meal on the go! Consider this for a fun picnic brunch.

Season chicken with salt, pepper, and chile powder. In a large skillet over medium-high heat, heat oil. Add chicken and cook until done, stirring occasionally, 5–7 minutes. Remove and keep warm.

In the same skillet, wiped clean, add butter. Sauté the peppers until tender, about 5 minutes. Add scallions and half cilantro and cook for 1 minute. Add eggs and scramble until softly set then fold in cheese.

Spread warm tortillas on a clean flat surface. Divide the chicken and eggs evenly among the tortillas. Spoon 1 tablespoon of salsa over each and sprinkle with remaining cilantro.

To finish the wrap, fold in the sides toward the center, fold up the bottom third, tucking the filling in as you roll up and keep rolling up until you reach the end. Use additional salsa on the edge to help seal the wrap. Place wrap seam side down and cut diagonally.

Vegetables
& Sides

Roasted Brussels Sprouts and Carrots with Pancetta

SERVES 8

This very colorful side dish goes with just about everything, is easy to prepare, and is full of nutritional value. Leave out the pancetta and you have a tasty vegetarian option.

Preheat oven to 400 degrees F. Line a large baking sheet with aluminum foil. Wash, trim, and cut larger sprouts in half, leaving smaller ones whole. Wash, peel, and slice carrots diagonally into 1-inch pieces to be the size of the sprouts.

In a large bowl, combine sprouts, carrots, garlic, pancetta, onion, salt, pepper, and rosemary. Sprinkle with olive oil and toss to thoroughly coat. Pour onto prepared baking sheet in a single layer. Bake 30–35 minutes, or until tender. Transfer to a serving dish and garnish with Parmesan.

2 pounds Brussels sprouts

1 pound carrots

6 whole cloves garlic, peeled

¼ pound pancetta, diced

½ red onion, diced

Kosher salt, to taste

Freshly ground black pepper, to taste

1 teaspoon dried rosemary

2 tablespoons olive oil

Grated Parmesan cheese, for garnish

Oven-Roasted Root Vegetables

SERVES 6 TO 8

1 large butternut squash, peeled, seeded, and cut into 1½-inch cubes

3 parsnips*, peeled and cut into 1½-inch cubes

4 carrots, peeled and cut into 1½-inch cubes

1 bunch beets, trimmed, and cut into 1½-inch cubes

2 small red onions, peeled and quartered

Kosher salt, to taste

Freshly ground black pepper, to taste

1 tablespoon herbs de Provence

2 to 3 tablespoons Garlic-Infused Olive Oil (page 23)

Root vegetables have great nutritional value and are a welcomed addition to any meal. The good news is that most root vegetables are available year-round. Mix and match them at your own whim. If you don't have access to herbs de Provence, substitute with a combination of your favorite dried herbs.

Preheat oven to 400 degrees F.

Spread vegetables onto 2 to 3 foil-lined baking sheets. Season with salt, pepper, and herbs. Drizzle with infused oil and toss to completely coat all vegetables.

Bake for 45–60 minutes, turning once, until tender and golden brown. Turn off oven and keep warm until ready to serve.

*If large parsnips are used, the tough core will need to be removed.

Collard Greens and Rice Casserole

SERVES 4 TO 6

Quick and easy to prepare, this is definitely a crowd pleaser. Prepare the night before and reheat in a 325-degree F oven before serving.*

In a medium pan over medium heat, bring rice, stock, butter, and salt to a boil. Lower heat, cover, and simmer until all liquid is absorbed, about 15 minutes. Set aside and keep warm.

In a large skillet or sauté pan, heat olive oil over medium heat and sauté onion until soft. Add garlic and sauté an additional minute. Add smoked turkey and collard greens and cook another 10 minutes. Season with seasoning and crushed red pepper. Combine rice and collard mixture in an ovenproof serving dish and serve.

*If reheated the following day, moisten with 1/4 cup of stock.

1 cup uncooked rice

2 cups chicken or vegetable stock

1 teaspoon unsalted butter

1/2 teaspoon kosher salt

2 to 3 tablespoons olive oil

1 onion, peeled and chopped

2 cloves garlic, minced

1 cup chopped smoked turkey wing meat

6 collard green leaves, washed and chopped into small pieces

1 teaspoon all-purpose seasoning

1/2 teaspoon crushed red pepper

Mediterranean Stuffed Tomatoes

SERVES 8

4 large vine-ripened firm tomatoes, stemmed and cut in half horizontally

Kosher salt, to taste

1/4 cup fresh breadcrumbs

1 large clove garlic, minced

1/2 cup grated Pecorino Romano or Parmesan cheese, divided

1/4 cup finely chopped fresh basil leaves

1/4 cup chopped Kalamata or Niçoise olives, optional

2 teaspoons extra virgin olive oil, more if needed

Freshly ground black pepper, to taste

This is the perfect accompaniment to any entrée—just the right amount of flavor without feeling overstuffed. For an easier preparation alternative, just slice the tomatoes, add the toppings, and grill.

Preheat oven to 400 degrees F.

Scoop out the pulp from the tomato halves. Salt insides and rest upside down on a baking sheet lined with a wire rack to extract juices, about 15 minutes. In a medium bowl mix, together breadcrumbs, garlic, 1/4 cup cheese, basil, olives, olive oil, and pepper. Stuff the tomatoes with the filling and sprinkle with remaining cheese. Bake until tomatoes are cooked through and tops are golden brown, about 30 minutes.

If cooking on the grill, the tomatoes will cook in 5–10 minutes. Watch carefully to avoid overcooking.

Roasted Stuffed Zucchini Boats

MAKES 8 SIDES OR 4 ENTRÉES

This is a great way to use the abundance of zucchini harvested from your summer garden, and it is an excellent vegetarian alternative.

Preheat oven to 400 degrees F. Wash zucchini and halve lengthwise. Cut a small slice down the back of each so they lay flat on a rimmed baking sheet. Using a small scoop, scoop out the middle flesh and discard. Spray or brush lightly with olive oil.

In a medium bowl, combine peppers, olives, scallions, mint, oregano, lemon juice, salt, pepper, and pepper flakes. Divide among zucchini halves. Bake until slightly tender but still firm, 10–12 minutes.

Turn on broiler. Top zucchini with feta and broil until cheese starts to brown, 4–5 minutes. Remove from oven and garnish with additional mint.

4 zucchini

3/4 cup chopped roasted red peppers

1/2 cup chopped Kalamata olives

2 scallions, thinly sliced

1 tablespoon chopped fresh mint leaves

1 tablespoon chopped fresh oregano

1/2 lemon, juiced

Kosher salt, to taste

Freshly ground black pepper, to taste

Pinch of red pepper flakes

1/2 cup crumbled feta cheese

Wilted Spinach and Arugula with Toasted Pine Nuts

SERVES 4

¼ cup pine nuts

1 tablespoon Garlic-Infused Olive Oil (page 23)

3 ounces fresh baby spinach, rinsed and drained

3 ounces fresh baby arugula, rinsed and drained

1 tablespoon balsamic or sherry vinegar

Kosher salt, to taste

Freshly ground black pepper, to taste

You can make this with all spinach or all arugula, but the combination of the mild and slightly bitter spinach paired with the strong and peppery arugula, is quite interesting. This is a dish that is made just before bringing it to the table. It cooks very quickly so make sure to have all ingredients prepped and nearby.

Place the pine nuts in a small sauté pan over medium-low heat. Let cook, shaking frequently, until fragrant and golden brown. Remove from heat and transfer to a bowl to stop the cooking.

In a large skillet over medium heat, add the oil. Add spinach and arugula and cook, stirring constantly, until slightly wilted, 1–2 minutes. Add vinegar and continue stirring until most of the vinegar has evaporated, about 1 minute. Stir in salt and pepper and gently toss in pine nuts. Serve immediately.

Fried Green Tomatoes with Aioli

SERVES 8

After summer is over and it becomes more difficult to source green tomatoes, try using tomatillos instead. They have a different flavor profile but are still very delicious and always available in the produce section. And their smaller size makes them ideal for plating up as appetizers.

Aioli Sauce

In the bowl of a mini-prep food processor, add egg yolk, lemon juice, and salt and pulse a few times to combine. With the processor turned on, slowly add the oil through the opening in the top until all used and sauce is thick. Add cayenne pepper and pulse a few more times.

Tomatoes

In a large shallow bowl, mix buttermilk with blackened seasoning. Add tomato slices and let marinate for 30 minutes. Line a baking sheet with parchment paper and a rack.

In a medium shallow bowl, combine cornmeal, salt, and pepper. One by one take tomato slices, shaking of excess buttermilk, and dredge in the cornmeal, making sure each side is thoroughly coated. Place on rack. Repeat until all tomatoes are coated.

In a large skillet over medium heat, heat oil about $1/2$ inch deep. Working in batches, fry tomatoes until golden brown on both sides, 2–3 minutes per side. Continue until all are cooked, adding oil as needed. Drain on a paper towel-lined platter. Serve with Aioli and garnish with scallions.

Aioli Sauce

1 large egg yolk, room temperature

$1/2$ lemon, juiced

Pinch of kosher salt

1 cup Garlic-Infused Olive Oil (page 23)

Pinch of cayenne pepper

Tomatoes

1 cup buttermilk

$1^1/2$ teaspoons blackened seasoning

2 pounds green tomatoes, sliced $1/2$ inch thick

$1^1/2$ cups stone-ground cornmeal

Kosher salt, to taste

Freshly ground black pepper, to taste

Canola oil, for frying, as needed

2 scallions, sliced

Southern-Style Succotash

SERVES 6

1 pound lima beans, fresh or frozen

6 slices thick bacon

1 Vidalia onion, chopped

½ cup chopped red bell pepper

1 large clove garlic, minced

1 cup ½-inch slices okra

3 cups corn kernels, fresh or frozen

Kosher salt, to taste

Freshly ground black pepper, to taste

3 tablespoons unsalted butter

1 pint grape tomatoes, halved

2 tablespoons sliced fresh basil (chiffonade)

Every Southern cook has their own favorite recipe and ingredients for this summer classic. But all will agree that two items it must have are lima beans and corn.

In a saucepan over medium-high heat, bring beans to a boil in enough water to cover by 1 inch. Reduce heat to medium-low and simmer until tender but not mushy, about 10 minutes. Drain and set aside.

In a large cast iron skillet over medium heat, cook bacon until crisp. Drain on paper towel, crumble, and set aside. In the same skillet with the drippings, cook the onion, bell pepper, garlic, and okra until onion is translucent, 3–4 minutes. Add corn, salt, pepper, and lima beans and cook for 5 minutes or until corn is tender. Add butter and stir until melted. Stir in tomatoes, basil, and bacon.

Sweet Potato Medallions with Currants and Pecans

SERVES 6 TO 8

These festive potatoes will pair very well with the Slow-Roasted Beef Brisket (page 140), Oven-Roasted Pulled Pork (page 126) or Honey Dijon-Glazed Ham Steak (page 128).

Preheat oven to 400 degrees F. Spray a 9 x 13-inch baking dish with nonstick cooking spray.

Arrange sliced potatoes in baking dish in 2–3 rows, at a 45-degree angle. (So that the slice in front is leaning on the slice behind it, and so on.)

In a medium saucepan over medium heat, combine sugar, butter, syrup, salt, cardamom, nutmeg, cinnamon, and vanilla. Stir until combined and sugar is dissolved and butter is melted. Continue to boil gently for 2 minutes without stirring. Remove from heat.

Pour sauce evenly over potatoes. Cover and bake, basting once or twice, for 30–35 minutes. Add currants and pecans and bake an additional 15 minutes or until potatoes are fork tender. Remove from oven, uncover, and let cool 15 minutes before serving.

4 medium-size longish sweet potatoes, peeled and sliced into 1/2-inch-thick slices

1 cup packed brown sugar

1/2 cup unsalted butter, cut into pieces

1/4 cup maple syrup

1/2 teaspoon kosher salt

1/2 teaspoon cardamom

1/2 teaspoon nutmeg

1/2 teaspoon cinnamon

1 teaspoon vanilla extract

1 cup currants or raisins

1/2 cup roughly chopped pecans

Cheesy Jalapeño Grits

SERVES 4

4 cups milk or water

Kosher salt, to taste

1 cup stone-ground grits

1 large jalapeño pepper,
   roasted, seeded, and small
   diced

2 tablespoons unsalted butter

2 cups grated sharp cheddar or
   Colby Jack cheese

*More than just for breakfast, these grits are made to stand up to more
complex flavors and meals. Use as a base for meats, fish, stews, and
hearty vegetables.*

In a large pot over medium heat, bring milk to a boil and add salt. Gradually
stir in grits and reduce heat to low. Simmer until grits are thick and creamy,
adding more milk if necessary, about 45 minutes. Halfway through cooking
time, once grits start to thicken, add jalapeños. Remove from heat and stir
in butter and cheese until melted. Taste and add more salt if necessary. Keep
warm until ready to serve.

Pasta & Casseroles

Boeuf Bourguignon

SERVES 10 TO 12

1 pound thick bacon slices, cut into 1/2-inch pieces

5 pounds beef chuck or beef tenderloin, cut into 1 1/2-inch cubes

Kosher salt and freshly ground black pepper, to taste

1 tablespoon olive oil

2 large onions, diced

4 carrots, halved and sliced diagonally

3 stalks celery, sliced diagonally

3 large cloves garlic, minced

1/2 cup cognac

1 bottle red wine (burgundy)

3 cups beef stock, more if needed

1 tablespoon chopped fresh thyme leaves

3 bay leaves

3 tablespoons concentrated tomato paste (in the tube)

6 tablespoons unsalted butter, room temperature

6 tablespoons all-purpose flour

2 tablespoons butter

2 pounds small mushrooms, quartered

1 pound frozen pearl onions

Fresh chopped flat parsley, for garnish

This traditional French beef stew has layers upon layers of flavor, like wine, cognac, and mushrooms. Served over pasta or mashed potatoes with a tasty vinaigrette salad and crusty bread, it is an impressive "go to" meal for any occasion. Halve this recipe for smaller gatherings.

Preheat oven to 350 degrees F. In a large Dutch oven over medium heat, sauté bacon pieces until brown. With a slotted spoon, remove to a paper towel-lined plate. Season the beef cubes with salt and pepper. In the same pot, working in batches, sear the beef cubes on all sides until brown. Remove to a bowl or platter and set aside.

Add the onions, carrots, and celery to the same pot and sauté until onions are translucent. Season with additional salt and pepper. Add garlic and cook another minute. Very carefully add the cognac, wine, and stock. Add the bacon and beef back into the pot, along with any juices that have accumulated. Stir in the thyme, bay leaves, and tomato paste. Bring to a low boil on top of the stove, cover, and transfer pot to oven. Cook for 2 hours until meat is tender.

While stew is cooking, make the *beurre manié*—a roux-like mixture of butter and flour used to thicken soups and stews. Using your fingers, spoons, or a few pulses of the food processor, mix the 6 tablespoons of butter and flour together very well. Drop a spoonful into your palm and roll into a little ball about 1-inch in diameter. Continue until you have several little balls. Set aside.

In a medium skillet over medium heat, add butter and sauté mushrooms until brown. Remove stew from oven and stir in mushrooms followed by beurre manié, 1 at a time, until desired thickness is reached. Add frozen pearl onions, cover, and return to oven for another 30 minutes. Taste seasoning one last time and adjust. To serve, spoon over favorite pasta or potatoes and garnish with parsley.

Breakfast Macaroni and Cheese

SERVES 6 TO 8

Mac and cheese is an "anytime of the day" meal or treat. But served for breakfast or brunch, on the same plate next to eggs, biscuits, and gravy, elevates this most beloved 'side' to center plate.

Preheat oven to 375 degrees F. In a large pot of salted water, cook pasta until al dente, 5–7 minutes. Drain and toss with 2 tablespoons butter. Set aside.

In a large saucepan, add milk, garlic, thyme, bay leaf, onion with clove, and mustard. Warm over medium-low heat until milk starts to steam, about 10 minutes. Remove from heat, set aside, and let the flavors infuse.

To a medium skillet over medium heat, cook bacon until crispy. Remove with a slotted spoon and drain on a paper towel-lined plate. Sauté jalapeño and bell pepper until soft. Remove and transfer to another paper towel-lined plate.

Strain the milk, discarding the solids. To a 10-inch ovenproof skillet over medium heat, add remaining butter and flour. Whisk for 3–4 minutes. Do not let brown. Whisk the milk into the roux to avoid lumps. Continue to cook, whisking constantly, until thickened, 3–4 minutes. Remove from heat and season with salt, white pepper, and nutmeg. Add the cheddar and Gouda and stir until melted then add the cooked pasta, peppers, half of the bacon, and half of the basil, stirring to thoroughly combine. You can bake this in the skillet, or transfer mixture to a casserole dish.

In a small bowl, combine Parmesan, breadcrumbs, and remaining basil and sprinkle over the top along with remaining bacon. Bake for 25–30 minutes until golden brown and bubbly. Let rest 15 minutes before serving.

1 pound cavatappi or elbow pasta

6 tablespoons unsalted butter, divided

4 cups whole milk

1 large clove garlic, smashed

1/2 teaspoon dried thyme

1 bay leaf

1/2 onion, studded with 1 whole clove

1 teaspoon dry mustard

1 pound thick-sliced bacon, cut crosswise into 1/2-inch pieces

1 jalapeño pepper, seeded and small diced

1 red bell pepper, seeded and diced

6 tablespoons all-purpose flour

Kosher salt, to taste

White pepper, to taste

Pinch of freshly grated nutmeg

3 cups grated sharp cheddar cheese

3 cups grated aged Gouda cheese

1 tablespoon chopped basil, divided

1/2 cup Parmesan cheese

1/4 cup breadcrumbs

Chicken Vesuvio

SERVES 4

1 to 2 tablespoons olive oil

1/2 teaspoon dried oregano

1 teaspoon dried thyme

1/2 teaspoon red pepper flakes, optional

1 whole fryer, cut up, or 4 bone-in, skin-on chicken breasts or thighs

Kosher salt, to taste

Freshly ground black pepper, to taste

1 pound baby red potatoes, scrubbed and cut in half

3/4 cup white wine

3/4 cup chicken stock

2 tablespoons unsalted butter

6 to 8 large whole cloves garlic, peeled and smashed

1 cup frozen peas

Fresh-squeezed lemon juice

Chopped fresh parsley, for garnish

This is an Italian-American casserole of bone-in chicken, potatoes, and peas that is easy to make for a pop-up brunch or a quick weeknight meal.

Preheat oven to 350 degrees F.

In a large Dutch oven or deep cast iron skillet, heat olive oil. In a small bowl, combine oregano, thyme, and crushed pepper. Pat dry chicken pieces and season with salt, pepper, and half of the seasoning mix. Cook chicken pieces until golden brown on all sides; remove to a platter. Season potatoes with remainder of seasoning mix and sauté until brown; remove to platter.

Add wine, stock, and butter and deglaze the pan, scraping up bits that have formed on the bottom. Add chicken and potatoes back into pan along with garlic. Bake, uncovered, for 45–60 minutes, or until the internal temperature reaches 165 degrees F on an instant-read thermometer. To serve, sprinkle with fresh lemon juice and garnish with parsley.

Grilled Eggplant, Tomato, and Pancetta Pasta

SERVES 4 TO 6

This dish could easily be made vegetarian by omitting the pancetta.

Preheat oven to 400 degrees F. On a large foil-lined baking sheet or shallow baking dish, arrange eggplant and toss with enough olive oil to coat. (Eggplant can soak up a lot of oil, so toss and let sit for a while before baking, adding more oil if necessary). Bake until cooked and slightly browned, about 25 minutes. Remove from oven and keep warm.

In a large deep skillet, cook pancetta until crisp and transfer to a paper towel-lined platter.

In same skillet over medium heat, add more olive oil and sauté onion until soft; add garlic and cook an additional minute. Add tomatoes, pepper flakes, salt, and pepper and reduce to medium low. Simmer 15–20 minutes until sauce is thickened and reduced to about 2 cups. Taste and add sugar if required to reduce acidity. Stir in basil and keep warm.

Cook pasta according to package directions and drain. Add pasta, pancetta, eggplant, and olives to sauce and stir to thoroughly combine. Serve and garnish with Parmesan.

2 eggplants, large diced (about 6 cups)

Olive oil

3/4 pound pancetta, thick-sliced and diced

1 onion, chopped

3 large cloves garlic, minced

1 (28-ounce) can fire-roasted diced tomatoes

1/4 teaspoon red pepper flakes, optional

Kosher salt, to taste

Freshly ground black pepper, to taste

1 teaspoon sugar, if needed

1/4 cup chopped fresh basil

1 pound penne, or other tubular pasta

1/4 cup quartered Sicilian black cured or Kalamata olives

Grated fresh Parmesan cheese, for garnish

Seafood and Chicken Paella

SERVES 10 TO 12

Paella is a well-known seafood and rice dish from Spain that gets its name from the pan that it is cooked in. Do not be rattled by the number of ingredients—the key to this dish is advanced prepping. Once started, the preparation goes very quickly.

This is the ultimate dish for feeding a crowd, but cut the recipe in half if preparing for a smaller group. If you do not have access to a paella pan, don't worry. Use a large ovenproof stainless steel or aluminum skillet instead.

3 tablespoons olive oil, divided

Kosher salt, to taste

Freshly ground black pepper, to taste

3 pounds chicken, bone-in or boneless

1 cup all-purpose flour (more if needed)

3 red bell peppers, seeded and chopped

3 medium yellow onions, peeled and chopped

5 cloves garlic, minced

3 cups Arborio or Spanish short grain rice*

3 tablespoons tomato paste

2 pinches saffron threads (turmeric may be substituted)

1 (14.5-ounce) can diced tomatoes, undrained

1 cup white wine

1 pound clams, littleneck or cherrystone

1 pound chorizo sausage, sliced ¼-inch thick

3 cups fish or chicken stock

1 teaspoon crushed red pepper flakes

1 pound colossal shrimp, peeled and deveined

1 pound mussels, cleaned and bearded

2 cups frozen peas, thawed

1 pound precooked crab claws

1 tomato, sliced in wedges

Red bell pepper strips, blanched

Chopped fresh parsley, for garnish

½ cup whole black cured olives or green olives

2 lemons, cut into wedges

(continued)

(continued)

Preheat oven to 400 degrees F. In a paella pan or very large ovenproof skillet, add just enough olive oil to cover the bottom and place over medium-high heat. Salt and pepper the chicken pieces and dredge in flour. When the oil is hot, add chicken and brown well. Transfer chicken to a platter and keep warm.

Add bell peppers, onions, and garlic to pan and sauté over high heat for 1 minute. Add remaining oil and rice and cook, stirring to coat rice evenly with oil until rice is slightly brown.

Stir in tomato paste, saffron, diced tomatoes, and wine. Return chicken to the pan and add clams and sausage. Add stock and red pepper flakes. Bring to a boil then place pan, uncovered, in the oven. Bake for 20–30 minutes, adding shrimp and mussels about 10 minutes before finished. Rice should be cooked, but still very firm. If additional cooking is needed to fully cook the rice, add more stock and return to oven.

When dish is done, remove from oven and stir in peas. Top with crab claws, tomato wedges, red pepper strips, parsley, olives, and lemon wedges.

Serve directly from pan, family style.

*Although the Spanish rice is preferred, it is more difficult to source. Arborio is an excellent alternative and is readily available.

Scallops, Mussels, and Shrimp Bucatini

SERVES 4 TO 6

This medley of seafood and shrimp is so delicious, and bucatini is the perfect "straw" for soaking up and diffusing the heat in the sauce.

In a Dutch oven or large pot over medium heat, heat oil. Add onion and scallions and sauté until soft, 3–4 minutes. Add anchovies and garlic and cook another minute. Stir in tomatoes, wine, oregano, basil, crushed pepper, salt, and pepper. Reduce heat and simmer until sauce thickens, 25–30 minutes. Stir occasionally. Cook pasta according to package directions. Drain and keep warm.

Increase heat under sauce to medium. Add mussels and cook for 3–4 minutes. Add scallops and shrimp, cover, and cook until opaque and all the mussels are open, another 3–4 minutes. Add pasta to the pot and mix well. Serve and garnish with additional basil.

2 tablespoons olive oil

1/2 cup chopped onion

1/2 cup chopped scallions

2 to 3 anchovies, chopped

2 cloves garlic, minced

1 (28-ounce) jar fire-roasted crushed tomatoes

1/2 cup dry white wine

1 tablespoon chopped fresh oregano

2 tablespoons chopped fresh basil

1/2 teaspoon crushed red pepper

Kosher salt, to taste

Freshly ground black pepper, to taste

1 pound bucatini pasta

1 pound mussels, washed and debearded

1 pound large sea scallops

1 pound extra jumbo shrimp, peeled and deveined

Chopped fresh basil, for garnish

Alfredo Seafood Lasagna

SERVES 8

This luscious white cream sauce pairs well with crab and shrimp. But feel free to add or substitute your other favorite seafood choices. Use this same recipe for making chicken lasagna. This is special enough for you to make it for any Sunday dinner or special occasion.

Heat oven to 350 degrees F. Cook noodles according to package directions. Drain and stir in 1 tablespoon butter to prevent noodles from drying and sticking together. Set aside.

In a large saucepan over medium heat, melt remaining butter. Add onion and cook for 2–3 minutes until tender; add garlic and cook an additional minute. Sprinkle in flour and whisk until flour starts to bubble. Do not let brown. Slowly pour in half-and-half, clam juice, and wine and whisk continuously to prevent lumping. Stir in salt and pepper. Bring to a boil and whisk for 1 minute. Remove from heat and stir in $1/4$ cup Parmesan cheese and parsley. Let cool slightly.

Into a 9 x 13-inch glass baking dish, spread $1/4$ of sauce. Top with 3 noodles and spread with half the shrimp, half the crabmeat, $1/4$ of sauce, and 1 cup mozzarella cheese. Repeat with another 3 noodles, remaining shrimp, crabmeat, $1/4$ of sauce, and 1 cup mozzarella. Top with final 3 noodles, remaining sauce, mozzarella, and Parmesan. Bake for 40–45 minutes or until cheese melts and top is golden brown. Let rest 20 minutes before cutting. Garnish with parsley and serve.

If made the day before, cover with aluminum foil and reheat in 350-degree F oven for 35–40 minutes, until internal temperature reaches 165 degrees F. Let rest for 15–20 minutes.

9 uncooked lasagna noodles

5 tablespoons unsalted butter, divided

1 medium onion, chopped

2 cloves garlic, minced

$1/4$ cup all-purpose flour

2 cups half-and-half

1 cup clam juice or chicken stock

$1/3$ cup white wine

Kosher salt, to taste

White pepper, to taste

$1/2$ cup grated Parmesan cheese, divided

$1/4$ cup chopped fresh parsley

1 pound cooked small shrimp, peeled and deveined

1 pound cooked lump crabmeat

3 cups grated mozzarella cheese

Chopped fresh parsley

Main Courses & Meats

Flavored and Spiced Bacons

MAKES 1 POUND EACH

As if it wasn't already the ultimate food in its own food group, bacon is taken to an entirely different level in these recipes. Experiment by stirring a slice into your Bloody Mary, crumbling into your favorite salad, or adding a few slices to your loaded cheeseburger or sandwich. It's bacon heaven no matter what way you do it!

Remove bacon from packaging and place on a large piece of plastic wrap. Do not separate slices. Generously sprinkle seasoning on the top and rub on evenly. Wrap tightly in plastic and store in refrigerator. When ready to cook, pull off desired number of slices and cook using your favorite cooking method.

Brown Sugar Bacon

1 pound thick-slice bacon

2 tablespoons brown sugar

1 teaspoon ground cinnamon

Honey and Pepper Bacon

1 pound thick-slice bacon

2 tablespoons local honey

2 to 3 tablespoons coarsely ground black pepper

Nashville "Hot" Bacon

1 pound thick-slice bacon

2 tablespoons Nashville "Hot Chicken" Seasoning mix

Breakfast Steak and Eggs on Asparagus Spears

SERVES 2

2 tablespoons Garlic-Infused Olive Oil (page 23), divided

10 to 12 asparagus spears (about 1 pound), trimmed

Kosher salt, to taste

Freshly ground black pepper, to taste

2 (5-ounce) steaks, of choice

Freshly ground grains of paradise or favorite steak seasoning, to taste

4 large eggs

1/2 teaspoon chopped fresh chives

Dash of Tabasco sauce

1/2 tablespoon unsalted butter

1/4 cup grated cheddar cheese

Sliced heirloom tomatoes, for garnish

Chopped fresh chives, for garnish

Whether its slices of leftover steak from the night before or a special 5-ounce breakfast cut from the butcher, steak and eggs is a hearty breakfast choice that will get you through the day. And the bonus is that you only need to use one skillet for the entire meal.

In a cast iron skillet, heat 1 tablespoon olive oil over medium heat. Season asparagus with salt and pepper and cook until tender, turning occasionally, 8–10 minutes. Remove to a platter and keep warm. Add remaining olive oil to the same skillet. Season steak with seasoning and cook for approximately 2 minutes on each side to desired doneness. Remove from pan, tent with foil, and let rest for 5 minutes.

Meanwhile, prepare eggs. In a medium bowl, whisk together eggs, chives, Tabasco, salt, and pepper. Wipe out the same skillet and melt the butter over medium heat. Gently scramble eggs to just under the desired doneness and remove skillet from heat. Fold in cheese. It is better to undercook the eggs than overcook, as they will continue to cook from the heat of the skillet.

To serve, arrange half the asparagus spears on 2 individual plates. Place steaks on top of asparagus, followed by eggs on top of the steak. Fan tomato slices on each side of plates and garnish with chives.

Grilled Prawns on Rosemary Skewers with Lemon Butter Sauce

SERVES 5 TO 6

If you are lucky enough to have an overgrown rosemary plant taking over your garden and have been wondering what to do with it, this recipe is for you. There are so many possibilities with this recipe. Alternate the prawns with sea scallops for an interesting combination. You can even wrap the prawns and/or scallops in prosciutto or very thinly-sliced bacon and add lemon or lime wedges to the skewer. You can't go wrong with this one—and did I mention how easy it is? This is also one of those summertime brunch entertaining ideas when you do not want to turn on the oven.

In a large bowl, toss prawns with seasoning, garlic, pepper, and enough olive oil to coat. Refrigerate for 1 hour. When ready to grill, heat outdoor grill to medium high.

Clean the needles off the bottom 2 inches of the rosemary skewers and thread prawns, approximately 5 to 6 per skewer, onto rosemary skewers starting at the bare end. Grill for 2 minutes per side until prawns are pink in color and the meat is opaque. Depending on the size of prawns, it may take an additional minute. Remove from grill and keep warm while you make the butter sauce.

Combine lemon juice, shallots, and salt in a medium sauté pan over high heat. Let reduce to half and add butter, constantly swirling the pan until the butter is melted. Add parsley and stir. Pour sauce over prawn skewers or pass in a small bowl. Garnish with lemon wedges.

Prawn Skewers

2 pounds colossal prawns or shrimp (usually under 15 per pound), peeled and deveined

Cajun or creole seafood seasoning, to taste

2 to 3 cloves garlic, minced

Pinch of crushed red pepper

1 to 2 tablespoons olive oil

5 to 6 sturdy (14-inch) rosemary sprigs, rinsed

Lemon wedges, for garnish

Lemon Butter Sauce

1/4 cup fresh-squeezed lemon juice

1/2 teaspoon chopped shallots

Pinch of kosher salt

2 tablespoons cold unsalted butter

Chopped parsley, to taste

Oven-Roasted Pulled Pork

SERVES 8 TO 10

Brining

¹/₂ cup salt

¹/₂ cup sugar

2 bay leaves

4 cloves garlic, smashed

2 tablespoons whole
 peppercorns

1 (5- to 7-pound) boneless
 Boston Butt (shoulder)

Seasoning

¹/₄ cup brown sugar

2 tablespoons smoked paprika

1 tablespoon chili powder

1 tablespoon garlic powder

1 teaspoon cumin

1 teaspoon kosher salt

¹/₂ teaspoon coarse black
 pepper

¹/₂ teaspoon cayenne pepper

You can't go wrong with pulled pork. Just put this on the table and watch faces light up. You don't need a slow cooker for this recipe—we cook it low and slow to get the best results. Brining the roast overnight will ensure that it retains its moisture and does not dry out in the slow-cooking process. This recipe works well with the Grit Cake, Collard, and Pulled Pork Sammie (page 83) or on a bun piled high with coleslaw.

Brining

In an oversize ziplock plastic bag or a large plastic container with a tight-fitting lid, combine salt, sugar, bay leaves, garlic, and peppercorns. Add just enough water to mix and dissolve ingredients. Place roast in bag and fill with enough water to completely cover. Place bag in a leak-proof container and refrigerate overnight, but not longer than 24 hours.

Seasoning

Preheat oven to 250 degrees F. Remove roast from refrigerator, drain, and pat dry. In a small bowl, combine brown sugar, paprika, chili powder, garlic powder, cumin, salt, and peppers. Rub mixture all over roast. Place roast on a baking rack inserted in a roasting pan. Insert an oven-proof thermometer in thickest part of roast.

Cooking

Place baking pan, uncovered, in oven. Bake until internal temperature reaches 200 degrees F, 8–10 hours. (Ideally, put in oven the night before serving and allow to slow cook through the night.) Remove meat from pan, reserving some of the baking juices, and wrap thoroughly in aluminum foil and let rest 30–45 minutes. This will also help meat retain moisture.

Using 2 forks, shred roast, place in a serving dish, and moisten, if needed, with some of the reserved baking juices. Serve with favorite barbecue sauce.

Honey Dijon-Glazed Ham Steak

SERVES 4

¼ cup honey

2 tablespoons brown sugar

1 tablespoon Dijon mustard

1 teaspoon ancho chile powder

½ teaspoon ground cardamom

1 bone-in smoked ham steak, ½-inch thick (about 1¼ pounds)

A ham steak is a nice alternative to cooking a whole ham, especially for a smaller group. Nothing leftover to hang out in the fridge for days while you try to figure out what to do with it.

In a bowl, combine the honey, sugar, mustard, chile powder, and cardamom.

Make diagonal cuts, 1 inch apart, on outer edges of ham steak to prevent it from curling up in the pan. Place the ham steak into a grill pan or large skillet over medium-high heat and brush the top with glaze. Cook for 4–5 minutes and turn over. (A grill pan will provide nice grill marks—great for presentation!) Brush cooked side with glaze and cook for another 4–5 minutes. Remove to a platter, brush once more with the glaze, and let rest for 5 minutes.

Shrimp-Andouille Grits with Okra

SERVES 4

Grits

3 cups milk

3 cups heavy cream, plus more for thinning if needed

1 cup stone-ground grits

It don't get any more southern than shrimp and grits . . . unless, of course, you add okra to it.

Grits

In a large saucepan over medium heat, add milk and cream and slowly whisk in the grits. When the grits start to bubble, reduce heat and simmer for 35–40 minutes, stirring occasionally to prevent sticking, until thick and creamy. Remove from heat and stir in butter, salt, pepper, and cheese. If still too thick, add additional cream, $1/4$ cup at a time until desired consistency. Set aside and keep warm.

Shrimp and Andouille

Into a large bowl, combine shrimp, salt, cayenne, and lemon juice; set aside.

In a large skillet over medium heat, add bacon pieces and cook until crisp. Transfer to a paper towel-lined plate and set aside. Add the bell peppers, onion, and okra to the skillet and sauté until onion is translucent, about 3 minutes; add garlic and cook an additional minute. Make a well and add sausage to the skillet and cook until brown.

Sprinkle the mixture with flour and stir; slowly pour in the stock and stir until mixture is smooth. When it starts to simmer, add shrimp and cook 2–3 minutes until opaque. Stir in bacon and 1 tablespoon parsley. To serve, spoon grits into individual serving bowls and top with shrimp mixture. Garnish with remaining parsley.

4 tablespoons unsalted butter

Kosher salt, to taste

White ground pepper, to taste

1 cup grated sharp cheddar cheese

Shrimp and Andouille

2 pounds medium uncooked shrimp, peeled, deveined, and tails on

Kosher salt, to taste

Pinch of cayenne pepper, more if desired

$1/2$ lemon, juiced

4 to 5 slices bacon, cut into $1/2$-inch pieces

1 red bell pepper, cut into thin strips

1 yellow bell pepper, cut into thin strips

1 onion, chopped

1 cup sliced okra, fresh or frozen

1 large clove garlic, minced

1 pound andouille sausage, cut into $1/4$-inch slices

$1/4$ cup all-purpose flour

2 cups seafood or chicken stock

2 tablespoons chopped parsley, divided

Lemon-Garlic Baked Cod

SERVES 4

This Mediterranean-style baked fish should feel right at home on any brunch table.

Preheat oven to 400 degrees F. Wash and pat dry fillets.

In a shallow bowl, whisk together 2 tablespoons lemon juice, $^{1}/_{4}$ cup olive oil, and butter. In another shallow bowl, combine flour, paprika, cumin, salt, and pepper. Dip fillets into the lemon mixture and dredge in the flour, shaking off excess flour. Set aside.

In a cast iron skillet over medium-high heat, heat remaining olive oil. Add fillets and sear on both sides until brown, but not fully cooked, about 2 minutes on each side. Stir garlic into the remaining lemon juice and drizzle over fillets. Transfer skillet to oven and bake 8–10 minutes until fillets are flaky. Remove from oven and garnish with parsley and lemon wedges.

4 to 6 cod fillets (4 ounces each)

4 tablespoons fresh-squeezed lemon juice, divided

$^{1}/_{4}$ cup plus 2 tablespoons olive oil, divided

2 tablespoons unsalted butter, melted

$^{1}/_{2}$ cup all-purpose flour

1 teaspoon paprika

1 teaspoon cumin

Kosher salt, to taste

Freshly ground black pepper, to taste

4 large cloves garlic, minced

$^{1}/_{4}$ cup chopped fresh parsley, for garnish

Lemon wedges, for garnish

Red Velvet and Pecan Waffles with Fried Chicken

MAKES 6 (8-INCH) WAFFLES

For the ultimate Southern holiday brunch at its best, build your menu around this combination. What's not to love?

Chicken

4 boneless, skinless chicken breasts, cut into 3 tenders each

2 cups buttermilk

¼ cup sriracha sauce

2 cup all-purpose flour

1 cup seasoned breadcrumbs

1½ tablespoons all-purpose or creole seasoning, divided

¼ teaspoon cayenne pepper

Canola oil, for frying

Waffles

2 cups all-purpose flour

4 teaspoons baking powder

1 tablespoon unsweetened cocoa powder

1 teaspoon kosher salt

¼ cup sugar

3 large eggs, beaten

4 tablespoons unsalted butter, melted

2 cups buttermilk, room temperature

2 tablespoons red gel food coloring

2 teaspoons vanilla extract

½ teaspoon white distilled vinegar

Chopped pecans, to taste

Homemade Sweet and Savory Bourbon Syrup (page 31)

Chicken

Place chicken tenders into a ziplock plastic bag and cover with buttermilk and sriracha sauce. Seal bag and make sure all pieces are covered with buttermilk mixture. Place plastic bag in a large bowl to prevent leaking and refrigerate overnight.

In another large bowl, whisk together flour, breadcrumbs, ¾ tablespoon seasoning, and cayenne. Before cooking, drain chicken in a colander for 30–45 minutes to bring to room temperature. Liberally season chicken with the remaining seasoning. Heat canola oil in a deep cast iron skillet over medium-high heat—oil should not come more than halfway up the sides of the skillet.

(continued)

(continued)

Working in batches, fry tenders until golden brown and temperature reaches 165 degrees F on an instant-read thermometer. Drain on a rack over a baking sheet.

Waffles

Preheat waffle iron according to manufacturer's instructions. In a medium bowl whisk together flour, baking powder, cocoa powder, salt, and sugar. In another bowl, whisk together eggs, butter, buttermilk, food coloring, vanilla, and vinegar. Add the wet ingredients to the dry and stir until combined. Allow to rest for 5 minutes.

Ladle the recommended amount of waffle batter onto the iron (according to manufacturer's recommendations) and add desired amount of pecans. Close lid and cook until waffle is golden brown on both sides and easily removed from iron. Keep warm in a 200 degrees F oven until ready to serve. Repeat until all batter is used.

To serve, plate waffles on serving plates, top with chicken tenders, and drizzle with syrup.

Homemade Rosemary Pork Sausage Patties

MAKES ABOUT 16 (2-INCH) PATTIES

These sausage patties are some kind of delicious! Make double batches to freeze and enjoy for several months. Also, you can use a few to add a flavor boost and moisture to your meatloaf and meatball recipes.

Combine all ingredients and chill for at least 1 hour or overnight.

Using the fine blade of a meat grinder, grind the pork mixture. Form into 2-inch round patties. Refrigerate and use within 1 week. If freezing, place patties on a parchment-lined baking sheet and put in the freezer for about 2 hours or until completely frozen. Then vacuum-seal or wrap tightly in plastic wrap and aluminum foil and keep in the freezer up to 6 months.

To cook, sauté over medium-low heat until brown, 10–15 minutes. If frozen, thaw overnight in refrigerator before cooking.

2 pounds pork butt, diced into small pieces

1/2 pound salt pork, diced into small pieces

2 teaspoons kosher salt

1 1/2 teaspoons freshly ground black pepper

2 teaspoons finely chopped fresh sage leaves

2 teaspoons finely chopped fresh thyme leaves

1/2 teaspoon finely chopped fresh rosemary leaves

1 tablespoon light brown sugar

1/2 teaspoon grains of paradise, nutmeg, or cardamom

1/2 teaspoon cayenne pepper

1/2 teaspoon red pepper flakes

Blackened Catfish on Herb Grits with Pineapple Relish

SERVES 4

Pineapple Relish

2 cups small diced fresh ripe pineapple

1/2 cup small diced red bell pepper

1/4 cup diced red onion

1 tablespoon chopped cilantro

1 lemon or lime, juiced

1 tablespoon honey

Grits

4 cups milk or water

Kosher salt, to taste

1 cup stone-ground grits

2 tablespoon unsalted butter

1 tablespoon chopped fresh parsley

1/2 tablespoon chopped fresh basil

1/2 tablespoon chopped fresh oregano

Don't panic when you see the end result of the cooked catfish—it's called blackened for a reason.

These herb grits provide that down-home base for this dish, while the pineapple relish smooths out the spiciness of the blackened effect. If this doesn't sound or taste like comfort food, what does?

If cooking indoors, remember to turn cooking fans to the high setting and open a window, as the blackened seasoning creates smoke. Due to the high cooking temperature, blackened dishes are best cooked in a cast iron skillet.

Pineapple Relish

In a medium bowl, combine pineapple, bell pepper, onion, cilantro, lemon juice, and honey; cover and refrigerate overnight. Bring to room temperature before serving.

Grits

In a large pot over medium heat, bring milk to a boil and add salt. Gradually stir in grits and reduce heat to low. Simmer until grits are thick and creamy, adding more milk if necessary, about 45 minutes. Remove from heat and stir in butter and herbs. Taste and add more salt if necessary. Keep warm until ready to serve.

(continued)

(continued)

Catfish

4 catfish fillets

Olive oil

¼ cup Blackened or Cajun
seasoning

2 tablespoons unsalted butter

Lemon wedges, optional

Catfish

Wash and pat dry fillets. Heat a large cast iron skillet over high heat. Sprinkle fillets lightly with oil and sprinkle generously with seasoning, shaking off excess. Add butter to skillet and when pan is sizzling, cook fillets for 2–3 minutes on each side. Remove to a platter and keep warm. Serve over grits and top with relish. Garnish with lemon wedge, if desired.

New Orleans-Style Barbecue Shrimp

SERVES 4 TO 6

Hot and very spicy, this shrimp dish is equally welcomed as an appetizer or a main course. This dish will not disappoint. Serve with lots of crusty bread to sop up the juice.

Clean shrimp and lay in a shallow casserole dish in a single layer. Melt butter in a small saucepan over medium heat. Remove from heat and let cool slightly. Add garlic, oil, Worcestershire, Tabasco, beer, lemon juice, cayenne, seasoning, paprika, black pepper, and herbs. Stir until beer foam subsides. Pour over shrimp, cover with plastic wrap, and refrigerate for 2 hours. Baste and turn shrimp every 30 minutes.

Preheat oven to 350 degrees F. Bake, uncovered, for 15 minutes or until shrimp are pink and opaque. Serve in soup bowls with sauce. Garnish with parsley.

2 pounds jumbo shrimp, peeled and deveined

1 stick unsalted butter

4 cloves garlic, minced

1/4 cup olive oil

1 tablespoon Worcestershire sauce

1/4 cup Tabasco or hot sauce, optional

1/2 bottle (6 ounces) beer

1 lemon, juiced

1 teaspoon cayenne pepper

1 tablespoon Creole seasoning

1 teaspoon paprika

1/2 teaspoon freshly ground black pepper

1 tablespoon chopped fresh rosemary

1 tablespoon chopped fresh parsley, plus more for garnish

1 teaspoon chopped fresh oregano

Slow-Roasted Beef Brisket

SERVES 10 TO 12

2 tablespoons brown sugar

2 tablespoons paprika

2 tablespoons kosher salt

1 tablespoon coarsely ground black pepper

1 tablespoon garlic powder

1 tablespoon onion powder

1 tablespoon dried parsley

2 teaspoons cumin

1 teaspoon chili powder

1 teaspoon cayenne pepper

1 (6- to 8-pound) brisket, trimmed

2 tablespoons liquid smoke, optional

Barbecue sauce, of choice

Brisket is to Texas what pulled pork is to the Southeast. The best brisket you will find is traditionally smoked or cooked low and slow on the grill so that it forms a crust—called the bark—on the outside. You can still get some of the desired results in the oven by using liquid smoke as one of the seasoning ingredients. The brisket is cooked wrapped tightly in foil but it is removed the last 2 hours to allow the bark to form.

Line a baking pan with heavy-duty aluminum foil. In a medium bowl, combine sugar, paprika, salt, pepper, garlic powder, onion powder, parsley, cumin, chili powder, and cayenne. Spread mixture generously all over brisket. (Leftover spice blend can be stored in a small jar in a cool, dry place for several weeks.) Sprinkle with liquid smoke.

Wrap in foil, fat side up, and seal completely; place in baking pan. If possible, refrigerate overnight. Remove from refrigerator 1–2 hours before putting into oven.

Preheat oven to 275 degrees F. Bake brisket for 5 hours. (Total cooking time will be approximately $1^1/_4$ hours for every pound.) Remove foil, pour off accumulated juices, and reserve. Return brisket to oven and cook an additional 2–3 hours. Brisket should be tender but not falling apart. Remove from oven and tent with foil. Let rest at least 1 hour before carving; cut into thin slices across the grain.

Desserts

Blueberry-Almond Puff Tarts

MAKES 18

Serve these tarts as a light finish to a hearty brunch or as just an accompaniment to a hot cup of joe. They pack easily and can go along on a picnic brunch. Feel free to substitute your favorite berries.

Preheat oven to 400 degrees F. Line 2 or more baking sheets with parchment paper.

On a clean flat surface, unfold puff pastry sheets. Cut each sheet along fold lines into 3 sections then cut each section into thirds. You should have 18 squares. Lay squares on baking sheets. Using a small paring knife, carefully cut a very small indentation all around the squares, $^1/_2$-inch from the edges but do not cut all the way through. This allows the sides to puff up higher than the center. Prick the center of the squares a few times with a fork, avoiding the edges.

Using a small spatula, spread cream cheese in the center of the squares, trying not to get any on the edges. Top the cream cheese with a few berries—it doesn't have to be exact and it is okay if the cream cheese shows through. Using a small pastry brush, brush the edges *very lightly* with the heavy cream. Sprinkle the squares with the superfine sugar. Bake for 15 minutes or until golden brown. Remove tarts from oven and sprinkle with the almonds. Let cool and sprinkle with powdered sugar.

1 package (2 sheets) frozen puff pastry, thawed according to package

1 (8-ounce) container spreadable cream cheese

1 pint fresh blueberries (can use frozen)

$^1/_2$ cup heavy cream

$^1/_4$ cup superfine sugar

1$^1/_2$ cups toasted sliced almonds

Powdered sugar

Lemon Curd and Gingersnap Trifle

SERVES 6 TO 8

Syrup

¼ cup sugar

½ cup lemon juice

¼ cup water

Lemon Curd

4 large eggs

4 egg yolks

1 cup sugar

1 cup fresh-squeezed lemon juice

1 tablespoon grated lemon zest

½ cup unsalted butter, cubed

Filling

2 cups heavy cream

1 (9 x 5-inch) plain pound cake

1 cup crumbled gingersnap cookies

When you find yourself with leftover pound cake and wondering what to do with it, here is your answer. And the results are pretty amazing. If your trifle dish is large, you may want to double the recipe. For a lovely presentation, try adding some flowers.

Syrup

In a small saucepan over medium heat, combine sugar, lemon juice, and water. Bring to a boil and cook until sugar dissolves, about 3 minutes. Remove from heat and cool completely. Set aside.

Lemon Curd

In a medium saucepan, whisk eggs and egg yolks together. Continue whisking while adding in sugar, lemon juice, and zest. Over medium-low heat, cook, stirring constantly with a wooden spoon, until mixture thickens and coats the back of spoon, 15–20 minutes. Do not let boil.

Remove from heat and stir in butter, 1 piece at a time, until smooth. Pour curd through a strainer, using the back of a spoon to help push through. Let cool to room temperature, stirring occasionally. Set aside.

Filling

In the bowl of a stand mixer with the whisk attachment, add cream and beat on high speed until stiff peaks form. Do not overbeat or cream will become butter.

(continued)

(continued)

Slice pound cake into thick 1-inch slices and lay on clean sheet pan. Using a pastry brush, brush slices on both sides with lemon syrup. Then cut slices in half or thirds.

Place half of cake in a glass trifle bowl or any straight-side glass bowl and spread half of whipped cream. Spread half of lemon curd on top of whipped cream and sprinkle with half of the gingersnap crumbs. Repeat layer, except for gingersnap crumbs. Chill at least 2 hours before serving. Sprinkle with remaining gingersnap crumbs before serving.

Chocolate Ganache

MAKES ABOUT 1 1/2 CUPS

8 ounces semisweet or bittersweet chocolate, cut into small pieces

3/4 cup heavy whipping cream

1 tablespoon cognac or brandy, optional

Place the chopped chocolate in a medium-size bowl; set aside. Heat the cream in a small saucepan over medium heat. Bring to just before a boil. Immediately pour the hot cream over the chocolate and allow to stand for 5 minutes. Stir with a whisk until smooth. If desired, add the liqueur at this time. Allow to cool until slightly thickened then use as a drizzle or topping.

Triple Peanut Butter and Chocolate Cheesecake

SERVES 12

This decadent dessert takes chocolate and peanut butter to an entirely new level. This is the ultimate brunch indulgence!

Crust

Preheat oven to 350 degrees F. In a medium bowl, combine crushed cookies, sugar, and butter and press firmly into a 9-inch springform pan. Wrap the bottom and outside of pan with aluminum foil.

Filling

In the bowl of a stand mixer, beat cream cheese and peanut butter for 3 minutes. Add both sugars and beat 3 minutes. Add vanilla and eggs, 1 at a time, then add sour cream. Pour into prepared pan.

Place cheesecake pan inside a larger pan and place in oven. Fill the larger pan halfway with hot water—this prevents the cheesecake from cracking or falling on top. Bake 60–70 minutes or until barely firm—center should still be shaky. Turn off oven, leaving oven door ajar about 6 inches, and cool for 1 hour. Remove from oven, remove foil, and cool completely in pan. Cover with plastic wrap and chill in refrigerator overnight or at least 8 hours.

Topping

Remove the side of springform pan. Arrange peanut butter cup halves over cheesecake, followed by peanut butter chips. Drizzle with Chocolate Ganache.

Crust

1³/4 cups crushed chocolate cookies

2 tablespoons sugar

4 tablespoons unsalted butter, melted

Filling

3 (8-ounce) packages cream cheese, room temperature

1 cup peanut butter, natural with salt and peanuts only

3/4 cup sugar

1/3 cup brown sugar

1¹/2 teaspoons vanilla extract

4 large eggs

1/3 cup sour cream

Topping

8 Reese's Peanut Butter Mini Cups, halved (more if desired)

1/3 cup Reese's Peanut Butter Mini Chips

Chocolate Ganache (page 146)

Rum—Chocolate Chip Pecan Pie

SERVES 6 TO 8

Bring this pie to the table at the end of the meal and you just elevated the occasion from eating to dining. You can never go wrong with serving a pecan pie! Just be sure to make two . . . and hide the second one for yourself to eat after company leaves.

Preheat oven to 375 degrees F. Place crust in a deep 9-inch pie plate. Cover crust with parchment paper and weigh down with pie weights or dry beans. Bake in the oven for 8–10 minutes. Remove from oven and remove weights and parchment. Allow crust to cool.

In a medium-large bowl, whisk together eggs, sugar, corn syrup, butter, vanilla, rum, and salt. Stir in pecans and $1/2$ cup chocolate morsels. Pour into pie crust and use a pie crust shield to prevent crust edges from burning.

Bake for 25 minutes. Sprinkle remaining chocolate morsels evenly over the top and cook another 20 minutes or until sides are firm, but center is still shaky. Do not overcook. Allow pie to cool. Serve at room temperature or slightly warm.

1 (9-inch) pie crust

3 large eggs

1 cup light brown sugar

1 cup light corn syrup

5 tablespoons unsalted butter, melted

2 teaspoons vanilla extract

3 tablespoons dark rum

$1/2$ teaspoon kosher salt

2 cups pecan halves

1 cup bittersweet or semisweet chocolate morsels, divided

Black Walnut–Cardamom Pound Cake

SERVES 12 TO 16

1 cup unsalted butter, room temperature

2 cups sugar

6 large eggs, room temperature

2 tablespoons almond extract

3 cups all-purpose flour

1/2 teaspoon baking soda

2 teaspoons cardamom

1/2 teaspoon kosher salt

1/2 cup sour cream

1 1/2 cups chopped black walnuts

Powdered sugar, for garnish

Not only is pound cake the hardest working dessert on a menu, it fits with whatever meal you are serving anytime of the day. Dress it up or leave it plain, its versatility is unrivaled. It goes equally well with ice cream, fruit, and sauces. Break it into pieces to make other desserts like trifle and tiramisu. You can even use it to make croutons, French toast, and brownies. The possibilities are endless.

Preheat oven to 350 degrees F. Spray a 12-cup fluted pan with baking spray.

In the bowl of a stand mixer, cream butter until it is a pale yellow. Add sugar and continue beating until thoroughly mixed. Add eggs, 1 at a time, and beat well after each addition. Add almond extract.

Mix flour, baking soda, cardamom, and salt together and add to butter mixture, 1 cup at a time, alternately with the sour cream. Fold in the nuts.

Pour into the prepared pan and bake for 1 hour and 15 minutes, until a cake tester inserted into the middle of the cake comes out clean. Let cake cool for 15 minutes in the pan then invert onto a wire rack and let cool completely. Sprinkle with powdered sugar to serve.

Quince Crisp

Quince is a member of the apple and pear family and is similar in appearance to both.

When cooked, the flesh changes into a coral pink color and it has the most incredible floral aroma. In the early to mid-twentieth century, quince trees were the cornerstone of most Southern vegetable gardens.

Topping

In a food processor, pulse flour, sugar, lemon zest, nutmeg, and salt until well combined. Add pecans and pulse just until they start to break apart, 2–3 pulses. Some whole pecans should still be visible. Add butter and pulse until mixture resembles a coarse meal with pea-size chunks. Transfer to a bowl and chill in refrigerator until ready to use.

Filling

Preheat oven to 350 degrees F.

In a large bowl, combine quince, cornstarch, lemon juice, bourbon, sugar, cinnamon, and vanilla until thoroughly mixed. Transfer filling to a deep pie or baking dish and cover with topping, spreading it evenly across the dish. Bake until topping is golden brown and firm and filling is bubbling, about 45 minutes. Serve warm or at room temperature with ice cream or fresh whipped cream.

Topping

1 cup all-purpose flour

1 cup sugar

1 lemon, zested

1½ teaspoons nutmeg

1 teaspoon salt

1½ cups pecan halves, toasted

12 tablespoons unsalted butter, cubed and chilled

Filling

8 quince, peeled, cored, and sliced

2 tablespoons cornstarch

¼ cup fresh-squeezed lemon juice

2 tablespoons bourbon, optional

¼ cup packed brown sugar

2 teaspoons cinnamon

1 teaspoon vanilla extract

Croissant, Pear, and Chocolate Bread Pudding

SERVES 8

10 to 12 croissants, cut into 1-inch cubes

4 large eggs

2¹/₂ cups heavy cream

1 cup sugar

1 teaspoon cinnamon

2 teaspoons vanilla extract

¹/₄ teaspoon kosher salt

3 to 4 pears, peeled, cored, and cubed

³/₄ cup bittersweet chocolate morsels

¹/₂ cup chopped walnuts

This recipe uses a well-loved brunch staple—croissants. With the addition of chocolate, the only thing that could make this better is a big scoop of vanilla ice cream on top.

Lightly spray a 9 x 13-inch baking dish with baking spray. Arrange croissant cubes in dish. In a large bowl, whisk eggs, cream, sugar, cinnamon, vanilla, and salt. Pour liquid mixture over the cubes. Cover with plastic wrap and refrigerate overnight to allow bread to absorb the liquid.

Preheat oven to 350 degrees F.

Remove bread pudding from refrigerator and gently toss in the pears and sprinkle chocolate morsels and walnuts over the top. Bake for 45–55 minutes until set in the center and golden brown on top. Allow to rest for 10 minutes before serving. Serve with a scoop of vanilla ice cream.

Baba Au Rhum

Cakes

1 tablespoon dry yeast

3 tablespoons warm water (110–115 degrees F)

3 large eggs, beaten

2 cups all-purpose flour

2 tablespoons sugar

1 teaspoon kosher salt

1/2 cup unsalted butter, room temperature

3/4 cup currants

3 tablespoons dark rum

Rum Syrup

2 cups sugar

1/2 cup apricot preserves

1 cup water

1 cup dark rum

1 1/2 teaspoons vanilla extract

Whipped Cream

2 cups heavy cream

2 tablespoons powdered sugar

2 teaspoons vanilla extract

Baba Au Rhum is a small yeast pastry saturated in rum syrup and served with a healthy dollop of fresh whipped cream. This old classic is making a comeback among brunch goers.

Cakes

In the bowl of a stand mixer, combine yeast and water and let rest for 5 minutes. Stir eggs into the yeast mixture.

In a medium bowl, combine flour, sugar, and salt and add to the mixer. And butter and, on kneading setting, knead for about 5 minutes until dough is soft and elastic. Cover dough with a clean kitchen towel and let rise 1 hour until double in size.

While dough is rising, soak currants in rum. When dough has doubled, fold currants into dough.

Preheat oven to 400 degrees F. Spray baba molds or 2 oversize 6-cup muffin pans with nonstick cooking spray. Spoon dough evenly into the 12 muffin cups. Cover and let rise another 30–45 minutes. Dough should have risen to the top of the cup at this point. Bake for 20–25 minutes until golden brown and starting pull away from the sides of the cups. Remove from cups and let cool on a wire rack.

Rum Syrup

In a medium saucepan over high heat, combine sugar, apricot preserves, and water and heat until sugar dissolves. Remove from heat and add rum and vanilla. Cool slightly. Dip babas, a few at a time, in the rum mixture and turn, to allow them to soak up the syrup. Transfer to a wire rack to cool completely.

Whipped Cream

In the bowl of a stand mixer with the whisk attachment, add cream, powdered sugar, and vanilla. Beat on medium-high to high setting until stiff peaks form. Do not overbeat or cream will turn into to butter.

To serve, place babas on individual dessert plates and top with whipped cream, or place on a large serving tray and allow guest to serve themselves.

Savory Spice Olive Oil Loaf Cake

SERVES 8 TO 10

This loaf cake is made with a surprisingly savory spice blend which includes rosemary and star anise. The result is a flavor that will make your palate very happy! It is excellent toasted and served with honey butter.

Preheat oven to 325 degrees F. Spray a 9 x 5-inch loaf pan with nonstick cooking spray.

In a medium bowl, whisk together flour, baking powder, salt, and spice blend. In a large bowl, whisk together eggs and sugar then incorporate olive oil, milk, rum, liqueur, and zest. Gradually add the dry ingredients to the wet and mix until thoroughly combined.

Pour into prepared pan and bake for 55–60 minutes or until a cake tester comes out clean. Remove from oven and let cool for 10 minutes. Invert onto a wire rack and cool completely. Dust with powdered sugar. Serve warm or room temperature.

2 cups all-purpose flour

1 tablespoon baking powder

¼ teaspoon kosher salt

2 teaspoons Savory Spice Blend

3 large eggs, room temperature

1 cup sugar

1 cup olive oil

½ cup whole milk

2 tablespoons white rum

2 tablespoons orange liqueur

2 tablespoons orange zest

Powdered sugar, for dusting

Savory Spice Blend

MAKES 2 TEASPOONS

Combine ingredients and store in a cool dry place until ready to use.

½ teaspoon Vietnamese cinnamon

½ teaspoon dried coriander

½ teaspoon dried oregano

¼ teaspoon dried rosemary

¼ teaspoon ground star anise

Tarte Tatin

MAKES 1 (9-INCH) TART

Crust

1¹/2 cups all-purpose flour

1 tablespoon superfine sugar

¹/2 teaspoon salt

6 tablespoons unsalted butter, cut into ¹/2-inch cubes and chilled

1 large egg yolk, chilled

2 tablespoons ice water

Filling

¹/2 cup unsalted butter

Pinch of kosher salt

³/4 cup sugar

7 to 8 Granny Smith apples, peeled, cored, and quartered

2 tablespoons Calvados, optional

This is an upside-down tart that has apples arranged in caramelized sugar with a top pastry crust. After baking, it is inverted and served fruit side up. A very simple yet elegant and impressive presentation.

Preheat oven to 375 degrees F.

Crust

In a food processor, pulse flour, sugar, and salt to combine. Add the butter and continue to pulse until mixture is like a coarse meal with some small chunks of butter still visible. Turn to the on position and add egg yolk and water and allow a smooth dough ball to form. If necessary, add more ice water, 1 tablespoon at a time. Wrap dough in plastic wrap and chill in refrigerator for 30 minutes.

Filling

In a 9-inch cast iron or heavy ovenproof skillet over medium-high heat, melt butter. Add salt and sugar and stir until dissolved. Cook until it caramelizes and becomes amber in color, 5–10 minutes. Remove from heat and arrange apples, rounded side down, in circles, packing tightly to cover all spaces. Drizzle with the liqueur.

Remove dough from refrigerator and let set at room temperature for 10 minutes. On a lightly floured surface using a floured rolling pin, roll the dough into a 10-inch disk. Place the dough over the apples and tuck into the pan around the edges. Using a fork, prick the dough all over.

Bake for 40–45 minutes until crust is golden brown. Remove from oven and let cool slightly. Carefully run a knife around the sides of the skillet and invert onto a serving dish. Cut into wedges and serve.

Brunch Cocktails

Pomegranate Mimosa

MAKES 4 COCKTAILS

This twist on the traditional mimosa is a refreshing treat anytime of the day, but it is especially festive for a special brunch.

Run a wedge of lime round the top of champagne flutes and dip flutes in the rimming sugar. Slowly fill each glass with 6 ounces of sparkling wine, followed by 2 ounces (1/4 cup) each of orange and pomegranate juice. Garnish with pomegranate seeds.

Lime wedges

Rimming sugar, optional

1 bottle chilled dry or brut sparkling wine, Prosecco or Cava

1 cup orange juice

1 cup pomegranate juice

Pomegranate seeds (arils)

Bellini

SERVES 1

Another brunch classic! The Bellini brings sparkling wine face to face with the peach, making it a winning combination.

Add purée to glass and slowly fill with Prosecco. Garnish with peach slice and mint sprigs.

2 ounces peach purée or nectar

Chilled dry Prosecco

1 peach slice

Fresh mint leaves

Chef Belinda's Creole Mary

MAKES 4 TO 6 COCKTAILS

12 ounces peppered vodka

24 ounces tomato juice

1½ teaspoons Worcestershire sauce

2 lemons, juiced

Pinch of freshly grated horseradish

1½ teaspoons Blackened Spice Blend (Chef Belinda Spices) or Cajun seasoning

6 lemon or lime wedges, for garnish

6 celery stalks, for garnish

One of the drinks that defines the brunch culture, the Bloody Mary, is purported to be the ultimate hangover cure. The blackened seasoning adds a new layer of flavor to this honored all-time favorite!

In a blender, mix vodka, tomato juice, Worcestershire sauce, lemon juice, horseradish, and blackened spice and pour into a pitcher. Cover and chill until ready to serve. Fill highball glasses with ice and use lemon or lime twists to flavor the glass rims. Fill with vodka and tomato juice mixture and add desired garnishes.

If using an unflavored vodka, add 1½ teaspoons Tabasco or dash of cayenne pepper to the vodka and tomato mixture.

Additional garnishes may include pickled okra or green beans, jalapeño or pepperoncini peppers, dill pickle spears, green olives, crispy bacon slices, seasoned boiled shrimp, and cherry or grape tomatoes.

Grapefruit, Champagne, and Vodka Spritz

MAKES 1 COCKTAIL

A spritz is a cocktail made with Champagne or Prosecco, a bitter liqueur, and soda water. Aperol is an Italian bitter aperitif, though sweeter and fruitier than its elder sibling Campari. Aperol gets its name from the Italian slang word apero, which means aperitif.

Into a tall wine glass pour Aperol, Champagne, grapefruit juice, and vodka. Add ice and a splash of club soda. Stir gently; garnish with grapefruit wheel.

1 ounce Aperol

4 ounces Champagne

1½ ounces grapefruit juice

½ ounce vodka

Ice

Club soda

½ grapefruit wheel, for garnish

Blood Orange Screwdriver

MAKES 1 COCKTAIL

Take the ordinary screwdriver to extraordinary—make it with fresh-squeezed blood orange juice. Another twist is to make it with grapefruit juice—and then it's called a Greyhound.

Fill a highball glass with ice. Pour in vodka and orange juice and stir. Garnish with orange slices.

Ice

2 ounces chilled premium vodka

4 ounces fresh-squeezed blood orange juice

Blood orange slices, for garnish

Cucumber Cooler

MAKES 1 COCKTAIL

3 slices cucumber

½ ounce Simple Syrup
(page 169)

1 lime, juiced

2 ounces vodka or gin

Ice

Cucumber slice, for garnish

There is nothing quite as refreshing as a cucumber—eaten alone, in a salad, or a few slices in a glass of water. Such a versatile ingredient, they are a great flavor booster when muddled in cocktails.

In the bottom cylinder of a cocktail shaker, muddle the cucumber with the syrup. Add lime juice and vodka, tightly cover with the lid, and shake. Strain over ice into an old-fashioned-style glass. If you don't have a cocktail shaker, a Mason jar does the trick. Garnish with a slice of cucumber.

Kir Royale

MAKES 1 COCKTAIL

1 tablespoon Crème de cassis

6 ounces chilled brut (dry)
Champagne

Fresh raspberries, for garnish

Crème de cassis is a black currant liqueur produced in Burgundy, France. It is mixed with white wine to make a Kir cocktail or with Champagne to make the Kir Royale, one of the easiest yet most elegant cocktails to make.

Chill Champagne flute in the freezer for 5 minutes. Add Crème de cassis and fill with Champagne. Garnish with raspberries.

Mint Julep

MAKES 1 COCKTAIL

4 to 5 fresh mint leaves

1 ounce Simple Syrup (page 169)

3 ounces quality bourbon whisky

Crushed ice

Mint sprigs, for garnish

Although considered the signature drink of the Kentucky Derby, the Mint Julep is more than just a one-trick pony! This front porch sippin' drink highlights the best of Kentucky's bourbon and is a delight all year long. To make it exceptionally special, don't forget the proper pewter cups.

Place mint leaves in a mint julep cup (a Collins or old-fashioned glass will also work) and add syrup. Muddle well with a long-handle spoon to release the oil in the mint.

Add bourbon and fill with crushed ice to the rim. Stir well until the glass becomes frosty. Add additional crushed ice, if necessary. Garnish with mint sprigs. Serve with a straw.

Bourbon Lemon Drop

MAKES 1 COCKTAIL

This cocktail is made with Limoncello, an Italian lemon-flavored liqueur made from the zest of special lemons grown only on the Amalfi Coast, Sorrento, and Capri. It is enjoyed alone, as an additive to cocktails, or used to make desserts.

Into a cocktail shaker filled with ice, pour bourbon, syrup, and Limoncello. Shake vigorously for 10 seconds and strain into a chilled martini glass. Garnish with lemon twist or slice.

Ice

2 ounces bourbon

2 ounces Simple Syrup (below)

1 ounce Limoncello

Lemon twist or slice, for garnish

Simple Syrup

MAKES APPROXIMATELY 1½ CUPS

Use in cocktails and nonalcoholic beverages requiring sugar.

Combine sugar and water in a medium pan over medium heat. Bring to a boil and stir until all sugar is dissolved. Let cool, jar, and refrigerate.

1 cup sugar

1 cup water

Index

Metric Conversion Chart

Volume Measurements		Weight Measurements		Temperature Conversion	
U.S.	**Metric**	**U.S.**	**Metric**	**Fahrenheit**	**Celsius**
1 teaspoon	5 ml	$^1/_2$ ounce	15 g	250	120
1 tablespoon	15 ml	1 ounce	30 g	300	150
$^1/_4$ cup	60 ml	3 ounces	90 g	325	160
$^1/_3$ cup	75 ml	4 ounces	115 g	350	180
$^1/_2$ cup	125 ml	8 ounces	225 g	375	190
$^2/_3$ cup	150 ml	12 ounces	350 g	400	200
$^3/_4$ cup	175 ml	1 pound	450 g	425	220
1 cup	250 ml	$2^1/_4$ pounds	1 kg	450	230

About the Author

BELINDA SMITH-SULLIVAN is a chef, author of *Just Peachy*, food writer, spice blends entrepreneur, and a commercially rated pilot. She has a culinary arts degree from Johnson & Wales University, and writes a monthly column for both *South Carolina Living* and *Bella Magazine*. She also is featured on *South Carolina Living*'s website with monthly how-to videos. Smith-Sullivan is an active member of the Southern Foodways Alliance, International Association of Culinary Professionals, American Culinary Federation, and Les Dames d'Escoffier. She lives in Trenton, SC.